The Year-Round Turkey Cookbook

A GUIDE TO DELICIOUS, NUTRITIOUS DINING WITH TODAY'S VERSATILE TURKEY PRODUCTS

Barbara Gibbons

McGRAW-HILL BOOK COMPANY   New York   St. Louis

San Francisco Auckland Bogotá Düsseldorf Johannesburg London Madrid Mexico

Montreal New Delhi Panama Paris São Paulo Singapore Sydney Tokyo Toronto

First McGraw-Hill Edition

3 4 5 6 7 8 9 MUMU   8 3 2 1

LIBRARY OF CONGRESS CATALOGING IN PUBLICATION DATA

GIBBONS, BARBARA.
    THE YEAR-ROUND TURKEY COOKBOOK.
    INCLUDES INDEX.
    1. COOKERY (TURKEYS)   I. TITLE.
TX750.G53   641.6′6′592   79-14889
ISBN 0-07-023161-3

BOOK DESIGN BY ANDREW ROBERTS

ACKNOWLEDGMENTS

WHILE IT MAY be true that too many cooks spoil a broth, a cookbook can't have too much help. This book wouldn't have been possible without the help of the turkey people, Louis Rich, Inc. of West Liberty, Iowa, especially Norman Rich, President, who initiated the project. For ready answers—usually on short notice and at odd hours—my gratitude goes to Stan Ullman, Director of Marketing, Dr. Charles F. Cook, Director of Food Technology, and Lisa Baum-Waters, Manager of Consumer Affairs, as well as Chris Boehlke and all the people at Daniel J. Edelman Public Relations in Chicago. My thanks for superb editing and design goes to Editor Tim Yohn and everyone at McGraw-Hill. Meanwhile, back on the range, my appreciation goes to my staff: Home Economist Dot Fast for getting it right (and secretaries Alvina Ostrowski and Moira McKaig for getting it done!). And finally, after all the testing, tasting and typing, thank heaven we all like turkey.

CONTENTS

PART ONE ▶

Introduction: Any Time Is Turkey Time

ONE THING today's turkey lover can really be thankful for is that our native American bird is no longer limited to once-a-year holiday visits to the family dinner table. It used to be that serving turkey was a major culinary event preceded by hours of cooking and days of preparation. And after it was all over, there was the big clean-up . . . and all those leftovers! It used to be that if turkey was what you wanted, a turkey was what you bought: the whole thing. Your choices were limited to big, bigger, and too big for the oven. Never mind that everyone in your family wanted dark meat, or didn't want dark meat, or that you had triplets who each wanted a drumstick to call his or her own.

Today, all that's changed, thanks to modern processing techniques. You don't have to wait for a crowd to gather to enjoy turkey—all kinds of turkey—any time you want. You can have dark meat—or never have dark meat—if that's your choice. There's no squabbling over drumsticks or wings or last parts over the fence, either. The wishbone is about the only sought-after turkey part that's not available in your supermarket, conveniently packaged in just the right quantity.

Besides being able to pick and choose your favorite parts, today you can choose turkey in forms that the Pilgrims—or your mother or grandmother, for that matter—never would have thought of. There are quick-cooking steaks and breast tenderloins for the short-order gourmet, ground turkey to make into meatloaf or pâté. Today, turkey can be lasagna or chili or tacos or hamburgers. You'll even find turkey hot dogs, turkey breakfast sausage, and turkey cold cuts: turkey bologna, salami, and pastrami with all the flavor (and a lot fewer calories) than their beef and pork counterparts.

What to do with this bonanza of turkey goodies that seems to be multiplying in your supermarket fresh, frozen, and processed meat cases? Most cookbooks offer little advice other than the usual time-temperature charts for whole bird roasting and make-overs for the leftovers.

Today's modern production methods make turkey available year round. Conveniently packaged for today's consumer, they are available both fresh and frozen. Once you have tasted fresh, you will understand why they are becoming so popular.

What's in Store . . . A Shopper's Guide to Today's Turkey

"Leaner Wieners™?" "Turkey pastrami?" "Turkey breast tenderloin?" Turkey thighs and breakfast sausage? Imagine how confused a Pilgrim would be if he could join you pushing a cart through a modern supermarket in any American city or suburb. My, how the Thanksgiving bird has changed!

If *you're* confused about the growing variety of turkey products available, here's a list to help. New products are being developed every day and not every product is on hand in every market. But this guide will give you some idea of the different products now widely distributed throughout the country—what they are made of, how they are packaged and sold, and how much to buy. (Serving sizes are based on U.S. Department of Agriculture data; the products described may vary slightly, depending upon the brand.)

Turkey products available at retail can be divided into two groups: "ready to cook" and "ready to eat" (fully cooked). The first classification includes all forms of raw turkey products that must be cooked before serving—whole turkeys, turkey parts, and ground turkey products. The "ready-to-eat" group is just that, already-cooked turkey products that are ready to serve as is, chilled, or gently heated through, if desired.

Ready-to-Cook

WHOLE TURKEYS: fresh or frozen, in sizes ranging from 5 to 25 pounds, natural or self-basting . . . some even come already stuffed! There is no significant difference in the flavor or tenderness of tom and hen turkeys (but tom turkeys tend to be larger, naturally). Turkeys self-basted with added fat or oil will have more calories per pound. According to U.S. Department of Agriculture data, whole, ready-to-cook turkey is about 27 percent bones, so you will need to allow two to three servings per pound (or two servings per pound for company and special-occasion meals).

TURKEY BREAST: fresh or frozen, a whole breast includes skin and bones and weighs 4 to 6 pounds. Extremely meaty, all lean and tender, this is the ideal no-fuss roast for white-meat fans. Some even have pop-up timers in them to indicate when the meat has roasted to its moment of perfection. Makes about three servings per pound.

TURKEY BREAST PORTION: fresh or frozen, weighing 2 to 3 pounds. This is half a tom turkey breast, including skin, bones, and part of the backbone; a versatile all-white-meat family-size roast. Makes about three servings per pound.

TURKEY BREAST HEN HALF: fresh or frozen, weighing 2 to 3 pounds. This is a turkey breast half, including skin, bones, and part of the backbone. A turkey breast half is an elegant all-white-meat roast that's perfect for small dinners. Makes about three servings per pound.

BREAST TENDERLOIN: fresh or frozen, this is a skinless, boneless, solid, fatless cut of turkey from the eye of the breast, weighing 8 to 12 ounces, generally sold two to five to a package; the "filet mignon" of turkey, waste-free, elegant, and exceedingly versatile. Makes about four servings per pound.

BREAST TENDERLOIN STEAKS: fresh or frozen. These are boneless, skinless, breast tenderloin steaks split lengthwise. They are very lean and tender, generally packaged four to six steaks to a package. Each steak averages 4 to 5½ ounces. Figure on one steak per serving.

BREAST SLICES: fresh or frozen, these are thin, boneless fillets (or "cutlets") of turkey, all white meat, cut from the breast—the "scaloppine" of turkey! Generally sold in 1- to 2-pound packages, each package averages five to seven slices. Makes about four servings per pound.

HINDQUARTER: fresh or frozen. This is a dark meat "turkey quarter" that includes the drumstick, thigh, and part of the backbone, plus skin and bones, weighing 3 to 4 pounds. A flavorful family-size roast for dark-meat fans. Makes about two to three servings per pound.

DRUMSTICK: fresh or frozen. This is the drumstick portion of the turkey leg, including skin and bone, generally sold two drumsticks to a package. Each drumstick weighs 1 to 1½ pounds. An economical choice for dark-meat lovers . . . very versatile. Makes about two to three servings per pound.

THIGH: fresh or frozen. This is the second portion of the leg, all dark meat with one center bone, and natural skin. Thighs are meaty and versatile, yet an economical choice. Usually sold one or two thighs to a package. Each thigh weighs between 1 and 2 pounds. Makes about four servings per pound.

WINGS: fresh or frozen. Wings are all white meat plus skin and bones, a budget buy. Usually sold two wings to a package. Each wing weighs 1 to 1½ pounds. Makes about two servings per pound.

WING DRUMETTES: fresh or frozen. All white meat plus skin and bone, this is the meaty first segment of the wing: miniature white-meat "drumsticks" with only one center bone. Sold in packages of four, about half a pound each. Makes two servings per pound. These are often called "wingettes."

WING PORTIONS: fresh or frozen. This includes the middle and wingtip sections of the wing, white meat plus skin and bones. Good for soups, stews, and stocks, versatile and economical. Usually sold in packages of four wing portions. Each portion weighs approximately half a pound. Makes about two servings per pound.

NECKS: fresh or frozen, skinless, all dark meat plus bones. Compared with those of other poultry, turkey necks are very meaty. They're an inexpensive choice for soups, stocks, and a good source of meat for salads, casseroles, and combination dishes. Generally sold five necks to a package. Each neck weighs about half a pound. Makes about two servings per pound.

GROUND TURKEY: fresh or frozen. This is dark or white turkey meat that has been ground like hamburger, but with a fat content usually less than 15 percent. (Ground beef can be 25 to 30 percent fat.) Ground turkey is a low-cost, low-calorie, all-meat "hamburger substitute" that can be used in many ways. Usually sold in 1-pound packages. Makes about four to five servings per pound.

BREAKFAST SAUSAGE: fresh or frozen. The sausage consists of dark and white meat, ground and lightly seasoned with spices; it is less than 15 percent fat (compared with 50 percent fat for pork sausage). Generally sold in 1-pound packages. Makes about eight breakfast- or luncheon-size servings per pound, or four dinner-size servings per pound.

SAUSAGE LINKS: fresh or frozen. Skinless links of turkey breakfast sausage are generally sold in 8-ounce packages of eight links. Each link is 1 ounce.

Ready-to-Serve (Fully Cooked)

The following turkey products are already cooked and ready to eat (or ready to *heat* and eat, if you prefer).

OVEN-ROASTED TURKEY: Boneless turkey white meat is lightly seasoned with salt and turkey broth for added juiciness, shaped for easy slicing, then oven-roasted to provide the flavor, texture, and appearance of home-roast turkey with no waste. Available sliced-to-order at deli counters, sliced and prepackaged in various sizes, and in solid unsliced packages or chunks. Slices average about 1 ounce each. Allow 2 slices for a lunch- or sandwich-size serving, 4 slices for a dinner-size serving. Also available as white and dark.

TURKEY HAM: Skinless and boneless meat from the "ham" of the turkey—the turkey thigh—is slow cured, then naturally hickory smoked and fully cooked to create an extremely lean ham with a fat content of 5 percent or less. Contains no pork or pork products and no added gelatin. Available sliced-to-order, sliced and prepackaged in various sizes, or in solid, unsliced 1-pound packages.

CANADIAN-STYLE TURKEY HAM: Slow-cured, hickory-smoked, fully cooked, skinless, boneless "ham" of turkey is shaped into 3½-inch diameter rolls. It provides the shape, taste, and appearance of Canadian bacon with a fat content of 5 percent or less. Allow 1 ounce for a breakfast side-dish serving, 2 ounces for a lunch- or sandwich-size serving, or 4 ounces for a dinner-size serving.

TURKEY BOLOGNA: Skinless, boneless turkey meat is cured, sometimes smoked, and cooked with bologna seasonings (spices and a hint of garlic) to create a deli meat with the taste and texture of premium bologna, but with a maximum fat content of only 15 percent (50 percent less than the standard for beef or pork bologna). Some brands contain no binders or extenders, no artificial colors . . . and no beef or pork! Available sliced-to-order at deli counters, sliced and prepackaged in various size packages, and in solid, unsliced 1-pound packages. Slices average 1 ounce each. Allow 2 slices for a lunch- or sandwich-size serving, 4 slices for a dinner-size serving.

TURKEY SALAMI: Skinless, boneless dark-meat turkey is ground and seasoned just like beef or pork salami, then shaped, cured, and naturally smoked with hickory to create a fully-cooked all-turkey salami with a fat content of only 15 percent or less (compared with more than 25 percent for "regular" salami). Contains no binders or extenders, no artificial color, and no beef or pork. Available sliced-to-order, sliced and prepackaged in various size packages. Allow 2 slices for a lunch- or sandwich-size serving, or 4 slices for a dinner-size serving.

TURKEY PASTRAMI: This deli meat is made from lean dark-meat turkey . . . instead of fatty beef plate. Lightly spiced with coarse black pepper, garlic, and other traditional pastrami seasonings, then shaped into a slab, turkey pastrami is slow-cured, hickory-smoked, and fully cooked to create an economical delicatessen meat that tastes like beef pastrami without the fat and calories. Less than 5 percent fat (instead of 42 percent fat for beef plate), turkey pastrami contains no binders or extenders, no artificial color . . . and no pork or beef. Available sliced to order, or sliced and prepackaged in various size packages, or in solid, unsliced 1-pound packages. Slices average 1 ounce each. Allow 2 slices for a lunch- or sandwich-size serving, 4 slices for a dinner-size serving.

SMOKED TURKEY: Skinless, boneless breast slices, breast halves, drumsticks, and drumettes are among the various smoked turkey parts and products now available at retail in some areas. These fully-cooked, ready-to-serve turkey specialties are lightly seasoned and naturally hickory smoked. Boneless sliced smoked turkey is available sliced-to-order, sliced and prepackaged, or in solid, unsliced 1- to 2-pound chunks (slices average 1 ounce each). Allow 2 ounces of meat for a lunch- or sandwich-size serving, 4 ounces for a dinner-size serving.

TURKEY FRANKS: Lean fresh turkey meat is blended with natural spices and seasonings, then naturally smoked to create skinless Leaner Wieners™ that offer more protein and less fat than ordinary hot dogs. Extremely economical, and they shrink less! Turkey franks have the all-American flavor of conventional franks without the calories and high fat content. They're a high-protein all-meat alternative to ordinary hot dogs, with no fillers or extenders, no artificial colors . . . and no beef or pork added.

PART TWO ▶

Today's Trim Turkey Is For Everybody

IF YOU "watch what you eat" you're not in the minority. In fact, if you're *not* calorie-careful—or cholesterol-, salt-, or nutrition-conscious—you're not in the majority of food shoppers! Jogging, salad making, label reading, and yogurt snacking are all testimony to today's preoccupation with revising our life style as a form of vitality insurance. Since most of us believe that we are what we eat, much of this scrutiny is rightly directed to what's on the end of our forks.

. . . which helps to explain the popularity of all those new turkey alternatives that keep on sprouting up in our supermarket meat case. After all, do we really need new kinds of hot dogs and pastrami made out of turkey when we still have the old kinds made out of pork and beef? Being less expensive doesn't explain why they sell so well in affluent, fashionable neighborhoods. What do the new kinds have that the old ones don't?

It's not what the turkey alternatives have—but what they don't have—that makes them so popular with body-conscious trend-setters. What pork hot dogs have, and turkey franks don't, is 500 additional calories per pound due to fat. And when it comes to fat, we definitely *are* what we eat!

Fat, after all, is the most fattening thing there is . . . more than double the calories of anything else, even sugar. Forty-five percent of our daily calorie intake is in the form of fat. Cutting down on fat—a chief recommendation of nutrition experts—is more than simply eliminating a few pats of butter or tablespoons of oil. Most of the fat we consume is hidden in the high-fat staples of the American menu: the inseparable fatty marbling in beef steaks and pork chops, and fat in a ham-and-cheese sandwich or in bacon and eggs, or in a hamburger and french fries. Not only lower in calories and lower in saturated fats than red meats, many turkey alternatives are lower in salt than their counterparts, turkey ham for example. Many of today's turkey products are nutritionally labeled, and you can compare the fat content for yourself.

Today's Turkey Is for Waistline Watchers

Everyone who's calorie-careful knows that turkey is relatively low in calories, but most diet-conscious cooks are amazed when they learn just how slimming turkey really is, not only in comparison to other meats, but even in comparison to other diet-safe protein foods. Check the chart on page 11 and you'll note not only that turkey products can save you considerable calories as an alternative to steak, hamburger, sausage, and lunchmeats, but also in comparison to such diet favorites as liver, cottage cheese, eggs, and shrimp. (And, in contrast to all these foods, turkey is exceedingly low in cholesterol!)

This cookbook shows figure-conscious food lovers how turkey can de-calorize everybody'd favorite meals. Turkey sausage, ham, and deli meats can stand in for pork sausage or bacon on your breakfast plate. Turkey franks, burgers, bologna, pastrami, or salami can take the place of fatty lunchmeats in your noontime sandwich. Turkey as the main ingredient on your dinner menu is a versatile choice for adventuresome cooks who can't afford to squander calories.

Today's Turkey Is for Hearty Appetites

Whether you have to pinch pennies or count calories, there's never a need to stint with turkey on the menu. Few foods give you as much appetite-appeasing protein in relation to both cost and calories. Americans have a big appetite for protein foods, but the problem with most meats is that the protein comes already "packaged" with a high fat content. Turkey doesn't. Hamburger contains 25 to 30 percent fat, while ground "turkeyburger" is less than 15 percent fat. Beef steak can be as high as 45 percent fat while turkey steaks contain less than 4 percent.

And turkey costs less. So whether you're watching your wallet or your waistline, turkey is a wise choice.

Turkey Is for Good Sports

Turkey is a high-protein, low-fat food that's ideal for the active life we lead today. Because it is protein-powered without the sluggish calorie counts and heavy fat content of most red meats, turkey is the energy food for sports-minded fitness fans. Turkey is a "good mixer": It combines well with fruits and vegetables in a variety of healthful dishes favored by health-minded cooks.

Today's Turkey Is for Busy People

Working parents and other busy job-goers are particularly thankful for today's easy-to-use turkey products. Turkey is the nutritious answer to "fast foods."

Many conveniently packed quick-cooking turkey foods can be table-ready in less time than it takes to thaw a frozen dinner or wait in line at a take-out place. Ready-to-eat turkey products that need no cooking can turn a sandwich, soup, or salad into an instant meal.

Today's Turkey Is for Singles . . . and Couples

Dinner for one, two, or a few is a snap with today's convenient turkey parts and products, available in just the right quantities for quick and easy solo (or couple) meals. Single swingers and senior citizens and others with tiny kitchens and limited refrigerator and freezer space are particularly grateful for the no-waste, small-space way that today's turkey products are packaged.

Today's Turkey Is for Big Families

Turkey is an affordable luxury, an economical choice that's especially smart for larger families. With today's turkey parts, the smart shopper can select his or her family's favorite parts . . . no debate over who gets dark meat or light! More-for-the-money turkey deli meats are especially good buys for the household with lots of lunchboxes to fill. In these days of shrinking food dollars, turkey steaks, turkeyburgers, and turkey franks are no-shrink budget-stretchers that offer better nutrition for less.

Today's Turkey Is for Tots and Teenagers

It's a food that's every bit as good for growing up as it is for grownups. Turkey's mild flavor and easy digestibility make it a good choice for young children. Even kids with fussy appetites ask for more when turkey is on the table. Turkey's versatility allows it to stand in for more fattening, less healthy ingredients in the foods that teenagers love. Burgers, hot dogs, chili, tacos, spaghetti, and hero sandwiches are extra nutritious, but nonfattening, when they're made with turkey products. Turkey can help teenagers be figure-conscious . . . without sacrificing nutrition.

Today's Turkey Is for Seniors

It's one of the good things that come in small packages, a wise buy that's relatively wastefree, economical, and easy to prepare. Nutritious, easy-to-digest and satisfying, turkey is also naturally low in fat, saturated fat, calories, cholesterol, and salt. Older people with special diet requirements will find many turkey choices to suit their nutrition needs. Adaptable to so many different dishes, turkey easily makes meals appealing to smaller appetites.

Today's Turkey Is for Particular People

Picky eaters are easy to satisfy with today's turkey variety. The shopper can choose exactly what the family wants, even if everyone at the table wants the same turkey part. And if everyone at the table wants something different, that's not a problem either. The wide availability of turkey in different forms means that the cook can pick and choose just the right type of turkey for every recipe. That's especially good news for the cook who hates leftovers!

Today's Turkey Is a Great Entertainer

It's the perfect partygoer that can fit into any crowd. Turkey is adaptable: familiar or exotic, depending on the occasion. It's a crowd pleaser that's both elegant and economical. The host or hostess with the least time to fuss will find that turkey's a perfect choice.

How Turkey Parts and Products Compare

The following chart compares turkey parts and products with similar foods. The protein, fat and calorie contents listed are per pound and per three-ounce portion of edible food (meat, or meat and skin or fat, without bones or other inedibles) without cooking, additional preparation or added ingredients.

Information on turkey parts and products was supplied by Louis Rich, Inc. Nutritive values for other foods are based on U. S. Department of Agriculture data (Handbooks Nos. 8 and 456) for foods commonly available in retail supermarkets.

	Grams of PROTEIN per pound	Grams of FAT per pound	CALORIES per pound	CALORIES per 3 ounces
ROASTS				
whole turkey breast	107	27	640	120
turkey hindquarter	85	64	960	180
beef rib roast	67	170	1819	342
loin of pork	78	113	1352	254

	Grams of PROTEIN per pound	Grams of FAT per pound	CALORIES per pound	CALORIES per 3 ounces
STEAKS AND CHOPS				
turkey steak	112	16	533	100
turkey tenderloin	112	16	533	100
beef sirloin	77	121	1420	266
lamb chop (rib)	69	138	1538	290
pork chop (center cut)	78	113	1352	255
CUTLETS AND FILLETS				
turkey breast slices	117	16	533	100
beef filet mignon	77	121	1420	268
beef minute steaks (round)	92	56	894	169
veal cutlet (scallopine)	89	41	744	140
liver (beef)	90	17	635	120
OTHER CUTS				
turkey drumsticks	96	21	587	110
turkey thighs	85	59	907	170
turkey wings	96	32	693	130
beef chuck	85	89	1166	219
beef shank	83	106	1311	247
lamb shoulder	69	108	1275	241
pork spareribs	66	151	1637	309
GROUND MEATS				
ground turkey	80	60	840	158
ground beef	81	96	1216	229
FRANKFURTERS				
turkey frankfurters	53	96	1067	200
all meat frankfurters	59	116	1343	253

	Grams of PROTEIN per pound	Grams of FAT per pound	CALORIES per pound	CALORIES per 3 ounces
BREAKFAST MEATS				
turkey breakfast sausage	56	64	880	165
pork breakfast sausage	43	230	2259	426
bacon	38	314	3016	569
Canadian bacon	91	66	976	184
ham (cured pork)	86	77	1061	200
COLD CUTS				
turkey ham	88	24	640	120
turkey pastrami	88	24	566	105
turkey salami	72	72	880	165
turkey bologna	64	64	880	165
turkey summer sausage	80	64	880	165
sliced smoked turkey	85	43	640	121
boiled ham	86	77	1061	200
beef (plate) pastrami	67	169	1814	342
pork salami	79	116	1411	266
liverwurst	74	116	1393	263
corned beef	72	113	1329	251
OTHER PROTEIN FOODS				
cottage cheese, creamed	62	19	481	91
cottage cheese, uncreamed	77	1	390	74
American cheese	113	46	1805	341
eggs	59	52	745	141
tuna fish, canned in oil	111	32	760	143
tuna fish, canned in water	127	4	576	109
King salmon, canned	110	79	1182	223
shrimp	82	4	413	78
lobster	77	9	413	78
sole and flounder	76	4	358	68
brook trout	87	10	458	86

PART THREE ▶

Turkey
Basics

ONE ▶ THE BASICS OF COOKING TODAY'S TURKEY AND TURKEY PRODUCTS

Any EXPERT will gladly tell you, there's only one proper way to cook turkey: his way. After that general rule has been established, the unanimity quickly dissolves into a debate over high and low temperatures, minutes-per-pound, what kind of pan, whether and when to baste, and if the turkey should be covered with a lid, cheesecloth, or foil. Or nothing at all.

We're here with the final, absolute, subject-closed last word on the question: The only way to cook turkey is the way that suits you best!

What way is that? It depends on what you want. Some folks like their turkey dripping with butter, while others are constitutionally opposed to one calorie more than is necessary. Some people *like* their turkey stewed in its own juices and falling from the bone, while others want a picture-pretty Norman Rockwell centerpiece, all crisp and golden and perfectly shaped. Some cooks consider turkey a failure if there are no pan drippings for gravy; others consider it a failure if there are. And yet, the way that suits you best may differ from time to time, depending on who's coming to dinner and when they're scheduled to arrive. If you're running late the best way—indeed the *only* way—may be the fastest way.

With all that in mind, we're ready to talk turkey!

How to Roast a Whole Turkey

Because roasting a whole turkey is generally a festive "come-to-dinner" company occasion, the method that's usually preferred is the one that will provide

16

the most attractive main course . . . that Norman Rockwell centerpiece we were just talking about. So these general directions are given with that aim in mind:

Thaw turkey if frozen. Here's the safest way: Leave the turkey in its plastic bag and place it on a tray in the refrigerator for 3 to 4 days (24 hours for each 5 pounds of dressed weight). Be sure to buy whole turkey enough ahead of time to allow for proper defrosting. If you're in a hurry, you may also defrost a whole frozen turkey in its plastic bag, completely submerged in cold water. Put the wrapped frozen turkey in a deep sink and fill with cold water. Change the water every 30 minutes. Allow 30 minutes defrosting time for each pound of dressed weight. Once the turkey is defrosted, cook it—or refrigerate it—immediately. If you plan to stuff the turkey, wait until just before roasting to fill the bird. (*Caution:* Thawing turkey at room temperature is *not* recommended because parts of the bird will become too warm.)

Prepare the fresh or thawed turkey by removing the plastic wrapper. Remove the neck and giblets. (Simmer them in salted water to make stock for flavoring the dressing and for giblet gravy, if desired.) Rinse the turkey in cold water; pat dry.

Stuff the turkey immediately before roasting, if desired. While a stuffed turkey is festive, your turkey will be "done" sooner, and can be roasted to a lower (and moister) internal temperature if you omit stuffing, or prepare a dressing and cook it in a casserole on the side. If turkey is not stuffed, you may rub salt or seasoned salt inside the turkey. For flavor, insert pieces of celery, carrots, onion, and parsley. If you do stuff the turkey, wait until just before roasting to fill the bird. Be sure that any meat ingredients used in the stuffing are thoroughly cooked (especially any pork products—pork sausage, for example). Stuff the turkey loosely; allow about ¾ cup of stuffing per pound of turkey.

Truss the turkey using white kitchen cord. Fasten the legs together with cord or tuck them under the skin band. Use skewers or cord to fasten the neck skin and wings to the body.

Place the turkey on a rack in a shallow roasting pan. For the most attractive turkey, place it breast-side-up. For moister white meat—and if the turkey is not too heavy to handle—you may place the turkey breast-side-down on a V-rack during the first half of the cooking time. Then, midway during the cooking time, turn the turkey breast-side-up, using a clean towel to protect your hands. Brush the turkey lightly with butter or fat, if desired (but this adds calories and isn't really necessary!)

Use a meat thermometer for best results. Insert the meat thermometer in the thickest part of the thigh, not touching bone. If the turkey is roasted breast-side-down during the first half of the cooking, you may delay inserting the meat thermometer until the turkey has been turned breast-side-up.

Roast the turkey in a 325-degree oven, following the time and temperature chart below. It is not necessary to preheat the oven. Do not cover the pan with a lid. You may baste the turkey, if desired, with any of the basting liquids listed

Time Chart for Roasting Turkey in 325-Degree Oven

Ready-to-Cook Weight	Approximate Cooking Time, Stuffed	Approximate Cooking Time, Unstuffed
6 to 8 pounds	3–3½ hours	2½–3 hours
8 to 12 pounds	3½–4½ hours	3–4 hours
12 to 16 pounds	4½–5½ hours	4–5 hours
16 to 20 pounds	5½–6½ hours	5–6 hours
20 to 24 pounds	6½–7 hours	6–7 hours

below. However, a "tent" of aluminum foil placed loosely over the turkey will eliminate the need for basting and prevent excess browning. Remove the foil during the last half hour of cooking for final browning.

Turkey is "done" when a meat thermometer indicates the following temperatures:

180–185°F whole stuffed turkey
175–180 whole unstuffed turkey
175–180 unstuffed turkey hindquarter or hindquarter parts
170–175 unstuffed turkey breast, breast half or breast portion

Despite the fact that most meat thermometers and cookbooks call for an internal temperature of 180–185 degrees, it is not necessary to cook unstuffed turkey to this high internal temperature. The 180–185 temperature traditionally called for is suggested primarily to insure that the stuffing is cooked through. But unstuffed turkey and turkey parts will be moister—and perfectly safe—at a lower temperature: dark meat is cooked through at 175 to 180, and white meat is moistest if cooked only to 170 to 175. According to USDA standards, turkey is "safe" once it is cooked to an internal temperature of 160 degrees or higher, but that is too rare for most consumer tastes. Consumer tests indicate that white meat is preferred when cooked to the 170–175 degree range, and dark meat is preferred at 175 to 180. We strongly suggest you invest in a meat thermometer and try our temperature recommendations.

Without a meat thermometer, turkey is "done" when the thickest part of the drumstick feels soft when pressed with the thumb and forefinger, and when the drumstick and thigh move easily. Protect your fingers with a napkin.

LET STAND 20 MINUTES—when turkey is "done," remove it from the oven and wait 20 minutes before carving, to allow juices to "set." Meat will be moister if you don't attempt to carve and serve it immediately.

See page 168 for directions to make dressing and gravy.

Low-Calorie Basting Liquids for Roast Turkey

Fat-skimmed turkey broth, made by simmering the neck in
salted water
Fat-skimmed canned chicken broth, undiluted
Reconstituted chicken broth made with boiling water and
bouillon
Champagne; sherry; dry vermouth; brandy; any dry white wine;
dry red wine (the alcohol calories evaporate)
Unsweetened cider or apple juice
Or, for variety, try these:
Tomato juice
Tomato-vegetable cocktail juice
Spicy ("Bloody Mary-seasoned") tomato juice
Unsweetened pineapple juice
Unsweetened orange juice
Any fruit juice, seasoned with soy sauce

Other Methods

The High-Low Method

Adherents of this method, used for whole roast turkey, claim that the
initial cooking at high heat seals in the juices and provides better flavor. There
will be a little more shrinkage, but the turkey will have less fat . . . and an even
lower calorie count!

Preheat the oven to 450 degrees. Prepare the whole turkey according to
general directions. Place the turkey breast-side up on a rack in a roasting pan.
Bake it uncovered in a 450-degree oven for 30 minutes, until the skin is crisp.
Drain and discard any fat; then lower heat to 325 degrees. To prevent overbrown-
ing, cover the turkey loosely with a tent of foil, cheesecloth, or a clean white
dishcloth dipped in water and wrung out. For best results, use a meat thermometer
to check internal doneness, and remove turkey from oven when thermometer
reads 175–180 degrees. Or, refer to the Time Chart on page 18 and deduct 15 to
20 minutes from the indicated cooking time.

The Slow-Baked Method

The away-all-day cook might like this method for whole roast turkeys, for
no basting is necessary because the turkey slow-bakes at a low temperature. For
safety's sake, this method is *not recommended* for a stuffed turkey.

Preheat the oven to 450 degrees. Prepare the whole turkey according to
general directions. Place the turkey breast-side up on a rack in a roasting pan.

Insert a meat thermometer. Place the pan, uncovered, in the oven and immediately lower thermostat to 275 degrees. Roast the turkey, uncovered, without basting until a meat thermometer reads 175–180 degrees (or about 20 minutes per pound). If your oven temperature is not true, bacteria can be a problem. For this reason, extra care must be exercised when using this method.

The Covered Roaster Method

As long as turkey roasters come with covers, people will continue to want directions for roasting whole turkeys with the cover on, even though a covered turkey isn't "roasted" at all, but steamed in its own juices. The steaming has the effect of drawing out the moisture, causing dryer meat and a somewhat shrunken and not particularly attractive bird. Are there any advantages to this method? Well, yes. You get a lot of delicious gravy! The skin is a lot softer, the turkey needs no basting, and it will cook in less time. This last point may be reason enough if you've got a crowd coming and you stayed too long at the football game.

To minimize the disadvantages of covered roasting, use the largest roaster that will fit in your oven, and keep the vent open all the while. (If the turkey is small enough and the roaster is big enough, you can almost create an oven inside your oven!)

Prepare the turkey according to the general directions and place it breast-side up on a rack in the roaster. Cover the roaster with the vent open and roast the turkey in a preheated 325-degree oven, allowing about 20 to 25 minutes per pound, or until a meat thermometer reads 175–180 degrees. Uncover and drain juices into a heat-resistant container; set them aside to permit fat to rise to the top. Raise the oven heat to 475 degrees and roast the turkey uncovered, just until skin is brown and crisp, about 20 minutes. Meanwhile, make gravy with the fat-skimmed pan juices. (See page 168.)

The Foil Method

Although this is a popular method, turkey cooked this way is actually "steamed" in its own juices rather than roasted. The juices are forced out of the turkey, which results in considerable shrinkage and less-moist meat. This method also requires longer cooking at higher temperatures because foil reflects the heat.

Preheat the oven to 450 degrees. Prepare the whole turkey according to general directions. Place the turkey breast-side up in the center of a large sheet of heavy-duty foil, shiny side up. Bring the foil up over the sides of the turkey. Fold the edges of the foil together; then overlap to seal them, so no moisture escapes. Place the wrapped turkey in a large, shallow pan, breast- (foil-sealed) side up. Insert a meat thermometer in the thigh through the foil, or roast according to the timetable below. Open the foil during the last 20 to 30 minutes to brown

WEIGHT	TIME AT 450 DEGREES (STUFFED OR UNSTUFFED)
8 to 10 pounds	3¼–4 hours
10 to 12 pounds	4–4½ hours
12 to 16 pounds	4½–5½ hours
16 to 20 pounds	5½–6½ hours
20 to 24 pounds	6½–7½ hours

and crisp the skin. Baste while browning with the juices collected in the foil, which will be considerable.

Not Recommended: The Paper Bag Method

Occasionally you may read or hear about roasting a whole turkey in a brown paper bag, a technique in which a whole bird is inserted in a big grocery bag placed on a pan in the oven. This method is not recommended! Many of today's grocery bags are made from recycled materials and may contain chemical contaminants which could be released by the heat and moisture of the oven.

The Rotisserie Method

This is a good method for roasting small turkeys in kitchen ovens with a rotisserie, or in hooded, motorized barbecues heated by charcoal, gas, or electricity.

Choose a small turkey, no larger than six pounds. Prepare it according to the general directions. Preheat the oven or barbecue. Center the turkey on the rotisserie spit and secure it with clamps. Use white kitchen twine to secure legs and wings to the body of the turkey. Insert the spit in the rotisserie motor according to manufacturer's directions. If oven roasting, place a shallow pan on a rack low in the oven to catch drippings. (Be sure the turkey will clear the pan as it revolves.) Turn on the rotisserie motor. Rotate and roast turkey at 350 degrees until done.

IN A COVERED BARBECUE WITH MOTORIZED ROTISSERIE: Preheat the coals (either charcoal briquettes or permannt "rocks") 20 to 30 minutes. Arrange the turkey on the rotisserie spit and turn on the motor. Close the barbecue hood. Timing will depend on the internal temperature of the grill. For best results, turkey should be checked with a meat thermometer.

HOW TO USE A MEAT THERMOMETER IN ROTISSERIE COOKING: After enough cooking time has elapsed to suggest that the turkey might be nearing doneness, turn off the motor. When the turkey stops revolving, insert a meat thermometer in the thickest part of the thigh. Close the hood or oven door and allow the turkey to continue cooking, without revolving. After 5 to 10 minutes, check the temperature reading. If additional cooking is required, remove the thermometer and resume the rotisserie action. Repeat this procedure until the turkey is ready. Turkey is done when the thermometer registers 175–180 degrees.

The Charcoal Method

In covered charcoal grill: form a "drip pan" from heavy foil, about the size of the turkey's length and width. Place the "drip pan" between two mounds of charcoal. Ignite charcoal, following package directions. When coals are ready, ash-white, place turkey on upper rack over the "drip pan." Close the cover and open all vents. Add additional coals after one hour. Charcoal grilling will take approximately 15 minutes per pound for unstuffed turkey; 20 minutes per pound for stuffed. Remove turkey when meat thermometer inserted in thickest part of thigh, not touching bone, registers 175 to 180 degrees for unstuffed turkey, 180–185 for stuffed turkey. Allow to rest for 20 minutes.

For other types of grills, follow manufacturer's directions.

Cut-up Turkey Parts

Techniques for oven-roasting cut-up turkey parts are similar to those for roasting whole turkey—except, of course, the cooking time is less. Preparation is simpler: There's no stuffing. A meat thermometer is recommended to take the guesswork out of timing.

Use a Meat Thermometer for Best Results

One of the advantages of roasting cut-up turkey parts instead of a whole turkey is that the turkey part can be roasted to the ideal temperature. White meat turkey (turkey breast, breast half or breast portion) will be moister if roasted to an internal temperature of 170–175 degrees, while dark meat turkey (hindquarter, thigh, drumstick) requires a slightly higher internal temperature: 175–180 degrees. So buy and use a meat thermometer for best results. Most meat thermometers indicate a higher temperature for poultry: 180–185 degrees, but you will find that today's young turkey parts are moister and more flavorful—and thoroughly "done"—if removed from the oven at a slightly lower temperature.

General Oven-Roasting Method

Arrange fresh or defrosted turkey breast, half, portion, or hindquarter skin-side up in a roasting pan. Season, if desired. Insert a meat thermometer in the thickest part, not touching bone. Place the pan, uncovered, in a 325-degree oven, and roast the turkey portion until a meat thermometer reads 170–175 degrees (white meat) or 175–180 (dark meat). Remove from the oven and wait 15 to 20 minutes before slicing. Discard any fat. While it is cooking, the turkey may be basted with a little broth, wine, or tomato or fruit juice, if desired. The average turkey breast will be done in about 2 hours. Dark-meat hindquarters take longer; allow about 2½ hours or more, until fork-tender.

The High-Low Method

Place the turkey skin-side up in a shallow pan in a preheated 450-degree oven. Roast for 25 to 30 minutes, until the skin is crisp and well rendered of fat. Drain and discard any fat. Lower the heat to 325 degrees. Season the turkey, if desired. Insert a meat thermometer in the thickest part. Roast the turkey portion at 325 degrees, until a meat thermometer reaches 170–175 (white meat) or 175–180 (dark meat). Baste while the turkey is cooking, if desired.

Basting Sauce Method

Follow the rule given in the High-Low Method (p. 19) to prebrown turkey. After the oven heat is lowered to 325 degrees, pour tomato sauce or any favorite sauce over the turkey. Spoon the sauce over the turkey occasionally while it roasts. Add water if the sauce evaporates too much.

To Defrost Frozen Cut-up Turkey Parts

Leave turkey in its plastic wrap and defrost it on a tray in the refrigerator 24 hours or more.

To Roast Turkey Parts Without Defrosting

Submerge the plastic-wrapped turkey in tepid water just long enough to allow easy removal of the plastic wrapper. Follow your favorite cooking method, but increase the roasting time about 50 percent. Midway during the cooking period, insert a meat thermometer in the turkey part or portion. (A meat thermometer is definitely recommended if you are cooking a turkey portion from the frozen state.) Note: This method may result in a tougher cooked product.

To Cook "Stuffing" with Turkey Parts

A small amount of dressing, about 2 cups, may be prepared and cooked in the same pan as the breast or hindquarter. Prepare the turkey and the dressing. ("Stuffing" should not be too moist.) Mound the dressing in the center of the pan and place the turkey, skin-side up, over it. Or, prepare any quantity of your favorite dressing and bake it separately in a covered casserole. (See Chapter 15.)

Basic Oven-Roasted Drumsticks, Thighs, Wings, and Wing Drumettes

SLOW-BAKED METHOD: Season the turkey, if desired, with salt or seasoned salt, pepper, and herbs. Arrange in a single layer skin-side up in a shallow nonstick roasting pan. Bake, uncovered, in a preheated 325-degree oven until fork-tender, about 2 to 2½ hours. Drain and discard fat. Baste with broth, wine, or fruit juice, if desired.

HIGH-LOW METHOD: Season the turkey. Arrange in a single layer skin-side up in a shallow nonstick pan. Bake in a preheated 450-degree oven 20 to 30 minutes, until skin is crisp and well rendered of fat. Drain and discard fat. Lower heat to 325 degrees. Continue to bake, uncovered, an additional 1 to 1½ hours, or until fork-tender.

Basic Braised Drumsticks, Thighs, Wings, and Wing Drumettes

IN THE OVEN: Brown the turkey pieces by placing them under the broiler, or by baking them, uncovered, in a single layer in a preheated 450-degree oven, until skin is crisp and well rendered of fat, about 20 minutes. Drain and discard fat. Put the browned turkey pieces in a single layer in an ovenproof casserole and add 1 cup of liquid (water, wine, tomato or fruit juice, canned tomatoes, or tomato sauce) plus any other seasonings desired.) Cover and bake at 350 degrees until turkey is fork-tender. If you wish, uncover the turkey and continue to bake until liquid evaporates into a thick glaze. Skim fat before serving.

Or, drain the cooking liquid into a saucepan. Skim the fat. Heat the liquid to boiling. Simmer, uncovered, until sauce is reduced to desired thickness.

Or, thicken the simmering liquid with a paste of cold water and cornstarch or flour (1 tablespoon cornstarch or 2 tablespoons flour with ¼ cup cold water for each cupful of sauce desired). If the sauce is too thick, thin it with a little boiling water. Taste and correct the seasonings before serving.

ON TOP OF THE RANGE: Brown turkey pieces by placing them under the broiler, or prebake the pieces, uncovered, in a preheated 450-degree oven until skin is crisp and well rendered of fat, about 20 minutes. Discard fat.

Or, you may brown turkey pieces in a large nonstick skillet or Dutch oven that has been prepared with cooking spray for no-fat cooking, with no fat added. Here's how: Spread the turkey pieces skin-side down in a single layer in the skillet or Dutch oven. Add 2 tablespoons of cold water. Heat the pan slowly over a low flame, until the water evaporates and turkey begins to brown in its own melted fat. Watch the pan carefully; turn the pieces frequently to prevent sticking. Drain and discard any fat. After the turkey pieces are browned, add 1 cup liquid to the pot (water, broth, wine, tomato or fruit juice, canned tomatoes, or tomato sauce), plus any other seasonings desired. Lower the heat to a gentle simmer. Cover the pan tightly. Cook very slowly until the turkey is fork-tender, 1½ to 2 hours. Check the pan occasionally and add water, if needed. Skim any fat from the cooking liquid. Then uncover and continue to simmer until the liquid is very thick. Or, thicken liquid with a paste made of cornstarch or flour mixed with cold water. Mix the paste well; then stir it into simmering liquid.

TO PRESSURE COOK: Follow top-of-the-range directions, but increase liquid to 3 or more cups. Reduce cooking time to 30 to 45 minutes. Follow manufacturer's directions for reducing pressure before opening the pressure cooker.

Pan-fried Turkey Breast Tenderloins, Steaks, and Slices

Use a nonstick skillet. To minimize sticking, spray the skillet well with cooking spray for no-fat frying. Add 1 to 3 teaspoons of butter, margarine, shortening, or oil. Heat the skillet over moderate flame. Rotate the skillet to spread the fat. Add the turkey in a single layer. Cook the turkey over moderate flame, turning once. (Cook tenderloins about 5 minutes per side; cook steaks and slices about 2½ to 4 minutes per side, until cooked through.) Season, if desired, after turning. *Be careful to avoid overcooking.*

Broiled or Barbecued Turkey Breast Tenderloins and Steaks

Tenderloins and steaks should be at least ¾ inches thick to broil; thinner slices should be pan-fried.

Preheat the broiler or barbecue. Put the tenderloins or steaks on a shallow nonstick broiler pan in a single layer. Spread the turkey lightly with 1 to 3 teaspoons of butter, margarine, shortening, or oil. Broil 3 inches from heat source (tenderloins about 5 to 6 minutes on each side; steaks about 5 minutes, on one side only).

NO FAT ADDED: Tenderloins and steaks may be marinated first in a sauce or seasoning liquid (wine, juice, salad dressing, and so on). Remove the turkey from marinade before broiling. Baste the turkey with the reserved marinade while it broils or barbecues, if desired.

Simmered Turkey Necks, Wings, Drumsticks, and Thighs

Put the turkey in a soup kettle and cover with water. Heat the water to boiling and skim any foam. Lower the heat to a simmer. Add 1 teaspoon of salt per pound plus any desired additional seasoning ingredients (onion, garlic, celery, parsley, herbs, pepper, MSG, wine, soy sauce). Cover the kettle tightly and simmer over very low heat until the turkey is very tender. Strain the broth and set it aside until the fat rises and can be skimmed with a bulb-type baster (or refrigerate until the fat hardens on the top of the broth). When the turkey is cool enough to handle, separate the meat. Discard bones (and skin, if desired). Wrap meat and refrigerate.

Ground Turkey and Turkey Breakfast Sausage

To cook, gently shape the meat into patties, *without* squeezing or pressing.

Panfry in a nonstick skillet or on a griddle prepared with cooking spray for no-fat frying (no added fat is needed). Cook 3 to 4 minutes on each side, depending on the thickness, just until cooked through. Season after turning.

Or, *broil* or *barbeque* 3 inches from heat source for 3 to 4 minutes on each side, depending on the thickness, until cooked through. Season after turning.

Or, use ground turkey or turkey breakfast sausage in place of ground beef in any favorite ground meat, meatball, or meatloaf recipe. It is not necessary to cook turkey sausage to render out fat. It is much better and juicier if it is not overcooked. Just cook to the point where the center is no longer pink.

Ready-to-Eat Turkey Products

"Oven-roasted," "barbequed" and "smoked" turkey products are ready-to-eat as purchased. They should be refrigerated. They may be served hot or cold. Because they are already cooked, there is no point in heating them any more than necessary. Continued or prolonged heating or too-high temperatures will only cause these delicious, tender turkey products to become less tender and less moist.

Ready-to-eat turkey breast portions, wing portions, thighs, or drumsticks may be reheated, uncovered, on a tray in the oven. Put them in a cold oven—uncovered—and set the thermostat at 350 degrees. It will take 20 to 30 minutes for the turkey to heat through.

Or, wrap the turkey tightly with foil, shiny-side in, and place the packet on a tray in a preheated 350-degree oven. The turkey should be heated through in about 20 to 30 minutes. (If you wish, unwrap foil to "crisp" the skin for last 8 to 10 minutes.)

The cooked turkey should be reheated with a little additional moisture to prevent the meat from drying out. Put the sliced turkey in a shallow pan and sprinkle it with a little water or turkey broth. Cover tightly and place the pan in a preheated 425-degree oven, just until turkey is hot, about 10 to 12 minutes or more, depending on the amount.

Or, heat turkey (or chicken) broth in a saucepan. When the broth begins to boil, lower the heat to a simmer. Add the sliced turkey to the broth and heat over a low flame for 2 to 3 minutes, just until turkey slices are hot. Sliced cooked turkey can also be gently heated in gravy or sauce. Sliced or diced cooked turkey can also be heated by adding it to other cooking foods in the last few minutes.

Turkey Franks

Like all franks, turkey frankfurters are cured and already cooked, so the only point of "cooking" is to heat them through. Because turkey franks are leaner, it's not really necessary to make slits in them to eliminate fat content (although you can make slits, if you like). However you "cook" them, turkey franks are ready-to-eat as soon as they are heated through.

TO STEAM: Put a rack in a pan and add 1 inch of water. (Be sure the water level is *under* the steamer rack.) Heat to boiling. Add the franks in a single layer. Cover the pan tightly and steam the franks 2 to 3 minutes, just until heated through. Or, for a "steamed" effect without steaming, heat water in a saucepan (1 cup for each frank). When the water boils, remove the pan from heat, drop in the franks, and cover the pan tightly. Allow the franks to rest in the hot water for about 10 minutes. Drain and serve.

TO PAN-FRY: Use a nonstick skillet sprayed with cooking spray if you'd like to cook turkey franks with no added fat. Or, heat a small amount of butter, margarine, shortening, or oil. Cook the franks over moderate heat just until heated through, 2 to 3 minutes. Turn them to brown evenly.

TO BROIL OR BARBECUE: Brush with oil, if desired (or omit oil to save calories). Broil or barbecue franks 3 inches from heat source, just until heated through, about 2 to 3 minutes. Turn franks to brown evenly.

TO COOK WITH OTHER FOODS: Turkey franks can be added (whole or sliced) to cooking foods in the last few minutes. Combine franks with sauerkraut, cabbage, beans, spaghetti sauce, or Oriental stir-fried vegetables. Cook only until turkey franks are heated through.

Ready-to-Eat Turkey Deli Meats

Turkey ham, salami, pastrami, and bologna need only gentle heating because these cured and smoked turkey deli meats are already cooked.

TO PAN-FRY: Spray a nonstick skillet with cooking spray for no-fat frying. Add the sliced or diced turkey deli meats and cook them over a moderate flame for 2 to 3 minutes, just until heated through. Or, omit cooking spray and use 1 to 3 teaspoons of butter, margarine, shortening, or oil. Don't overcook.

TO BROIL OR BARBECUE: Purchase turkey deli meats unsliced. Slice or dice at least 1 inch thick. (Presliced meats are sliced too thin for broiling and are better pan-fried.) Broil or barbecue 3 inches from heat source, turning to brown evenly. Cook only 2 to 3 minutes, just until heated through.

IN THE OVEN: Wrap sliced turkey deli meat in a foil packet. Bake in a preheated 350-degree oven about 10 to 15 minutes, just until heated through.

IN A MICROWAVE OVEN: Cooking time depends on the quantity of meat and the wattage of the setting. Two ounces of sliced turkey deli meats will heat in less than 20 seconds. Watch the meat carefully and turn off the microwave oven as soon as meat begins to steam.

TO COOK WITH OTHER FOODS: Diced or sliced turkey deli meats may be added to other foods in the last few minutes of cooking. Combine them with cooking foods over low heat. Cook 2 to 3 minutes; remove the food from the heat as soon as the meat is heated through.

PART FOUR ▶

The
Recipes

ONE ▶ TURKEY WITH
A FOREIGN FLAVOR

Our NATIVE American bird is a sophisticated world traveler that adapts easily to the cuisines of other countries. That's good news for adventuresome cooks—particularly those who are cost- or calorie-conscious as well as nutrition-wise. Turkey can stand in for more expensive, less nutritious meats and cut calories at the same time. Whether your taste in foreign foods run to hearty, highly seasoned "ethnic" dishes or elegant cosmopolitan cuisine, you'll find that cooking with a foreign flavor needn't be fattening . . . *if* you make it with turkey!

What makes turkey such a self-assured traveler in the cuisines of other countries is its easy adaptability to spices and seasonings . . . and seasoning is what ethnic cooking is all about! "Flavor" doesn't have to depend on fat. Herbs and spices have no calories to speak of. Most of the real "flavor-makers" that give a dish its foreign accent contribute relatively little to the calorie count, whether it's a zesty blend of garlic and tomatoes, a subtle spicing of nutmeg and wine, the bite of hot pepper or horseradish, or the savory fragrance of mint or thyme.

Here are some ways that turkey makes it easy to cook with a foreign accent:

▶ Lean cubes of turkey cut from the thigh can take the place of those high-fat beef cuts generally called for in slow-simmered ethnic stews and ragouts. (In these dishes the meat cooks in its own sauce, so the fat content is an inescapable addition to the caloric bottom line!)

▶ Tender slices from the breast of turkey can stand in for the far-more-costly veal that's a favorite in continental cuisine. Like veal, turkey is equally at home with the lemon, garlic, onions, and tomatoes of Italian cookery . . . and the subtly seasoned, wine-spiked sauces of French cuisine.

▶ Dark-meat turkey is the always-available replacement for the often hard-to-find lamb that's a favorite in Greek and Middle Eastern dishes. Like lamb, turkey is at home with exotic seasonings and spices.

▶ White-meat turkey can substitute for the much-more-fattening pork that's popular in Chinese and Polynesian dishes. Bite-size cubes of turkey stir-fry quickly with crisp Oriental vegetables.

▶ Duck, a favorite-but-fattening choice in many Oriental recipes, can be replaced by dark-meat turkey from the thigh or hindquarter.

▶ Ground turkey adds a new dimension to any dish normally made with hamburger, whether it's a kid-pleasing lasagna or a party-going pâté. Turkey can combine with other ground meats to make marvelous meatloaves with less fat and fewer calories.

▶ With its mild flavor, turkey pairs perfectly with spicy ingredients in everybody's favorite "hot" cuisines: Mexican chilis, Indian curries, and Szechuan-style Oriental dishes are doubly delicious made with turkey.

▶ Turkey deli products can come to the rescue when ethnic favorites are off-limits because they call for pastrami, bologna, salami, ham, or frankfurters. The turkey versions of these cured meats are only a fraction of the usual calories.

In putting together this collection of turkey dishes with foreign flavor, we've tried to incorporate cooking techniques that eliminate fat rather than add it, and used ingredients that are naturally high in nutrition while relatively calorie-shy.

Turkey Rouladen

1 pound (8) raw turkey breast slices
1 tablespoon prepared mustard (mild or hot, to taste)
  Salt and pepper to taste
⅛ teaspoon marjoram
1 small minced onion
2 dill pickles, quartered lengthwise (into spears)
1 tablespoon butter or margarine
1¼ cups fat-skimmed turkey broth
1½ tablespoons flour
  Fresh parsley

Lay each turkey slice flat on a cutting board. Spread lightly with mustard. Season with salt and pepper. Sprinkle with marjoram and onion. Put one pickle spear on top of each turkey slice. Then roll turkey around pickle and secure with a toothpick.

Spray a nonstick skillet with cooking spray for no-fat frying. Melt the butter or margarine. Brown the rouladen over medium heat, turning to brown evenly. Add 1 cup of the broth. Cover and simmer over low heat until tender, about 10 minutes.

Remove rouladen to a platter and keep warm. Remove toothpicks. Combine remaining ¼ cup of broth with flour and stir into pan liquid. Cook over low heat, stirring, until sauce is thick. Spoon over rouladen and serve immediately. Garnish with parsley.

Makes four servings, about 205 calories each.

Israeli Roast Turkey Tarragon

1 turkey breast (4 to 6 pounds)
½ cup lemon juice
1 cup orange juice
2 teaspoons grated lemon or orange peel
1 teaspoon crushed tarragon
  Salt or garlic salt, pepper, and paprika to taste

Place turkey breast skin-side up in a shallow roasting pan. Bake in preheated 450-degree oven 20 to 30 minutes, until skin is crisp and well rendered of fat. Drain and discard any fat.

Combine citrus juices, peel, and tarragon; pour over turkey. Sprinkle with salt, pepper, and paprika to taste. Lower oven heat to 325 degrees. Bake, basting occasionally, until turkey is tender, or until a meat thermometer reads 185 degrees. Spoon sauce over turkey to serve.

Each four-ounce serving, about 180 calories.

Turkey Souvlakia

5 tablespoons low-fat Italian salad dressing
  Pinch of nutmeg
  Pinch of instant garlic
1 teaspoon dried mint

Mix salad dressing with nutmeg, garlic, and mint. Marinate cooked turkey cubes in the mixture covered in the refrigerator for several hours.

Thread turkey cubes on skewers, alternating with vegetables. Add oil to the remaining marinade,

1 pound cooked turkey breast
   tenderloin, cut into 1-inch
   cubes
4 seeded red and green bell peppers,
   cut into squares
4 small peeled, quartered onions
1 zucchini, cut into 1-inch cubes
2 teaspoons salad oil

then brush combined mixture on skewers. Broil or barbecue 2 inches from heat source for about 5 minutes on each side, just until seared and heated through. Vegetables should be hot but crunchy.

Makes four servings, about 250 calories each.

Turkey Cantonese

½ cup chicken or turkey broth (fat
   skimmed)
1 clove grated garlic
½ cup pineapple juice
1 pound julienned turkey breast
   slices
2 medium Spanish onions, halved
   and sliced
2 chopped green bell peppers
2 chopped red bell peppers
4 tablespoons soy sauce
   Pinch of anise seed or fennel seed

Combine the broth, garlic and pineapple juice in a wok or large frying pan and bring to a boil. Boil for 10 to 15 minutes to reduce liquid. Julienne turkey breast slices and place in the wok; stir fry for 10 minutes. Add the sliced onions, peppers, soy sauce and anise seed. Stir and cook for an additional 4 minutes. (Serve on a bed of rice, if desired.)

Makes 5 servings, about 160 calories each.

Turkey Parmigiana

1 egg or 2 egg whites or ¼ cup
   defrosted no-cholesterol
   substitute
2 tablespoons salad oil
1 pound turkey breast slices
⅓ cup seasoned dry bread crumbs
½ teaspoon salt
   dash pepper
3 ounces tomato paste
¾ cup fat-skimmed turkey or chicken
   broth
1 clove minced garlic
1 teaspoon oregano
4 ounces part-skimmed Mozzarella
   cheese
   shredded parsley

Fork-blend the egg and the oil. Dip the turkey breast slices into egg mixture, then coat both sides lightly with the bread crumbs. Arrange the turkey in a single layer on a cookie sheet prepared with non-stick spray. Bake 8 to 10 minutes at 450 degrees until golden and crisp. Do not turn. Transfer to an oven-proof platter.

Combine the salt, pepper, tomato paste, broth, garlic and oregano. Simmer uncovered over moderate heat until thickened, then spoon over the turkey. Top with cheese, then broil until cheese bubbles. Garnish with parsley.

Makes four servings, about 275 calories each (10 calories less per serving with egg whites or substitute).

Israeli Turkey Fillets

1 pound turkey tenderloin steaks
2 tablespoons lemon juice
½ teaspoon ground cumin
¼ teaspoon liquid hot pepper sauce
    (or more, to taste)
    Paprika
2 teaspoons olive oil

Arrange turkey steaks in a single layer on a platter. Combine lemon juice, cumin, and pepper sauce, and spread over steaks. Sprinkle with paprika.

Cover and refrigerate several hours. Heat oil in a nonstick skillet. Pan-fry steaks over moderate heat, 2½ to 4 minutes per side, turning once.

Makes four servings, about 155 calories each.

Turkey Irish Stew

2 skinned, boned turkey thighs, cut
    into 1-inch cubes
4 peeled, diced potatoes
2 peeled, sliced onions
4 scraped, sliced carrots
¼ cup dry white wine or water
    optional: 1 bay leaf
    Salt and pepper to taste

Combine all ingredients in crockpot or slow-cooker. Heat on high heat until simmering; then lower to slow-cook setting. Cook covered, 8 to 10 hours, according to manufacturer's directions.

Makes ten servings, about 325 calories each.

Turkey Adobo

1 turkey thigh
1 seeded, diced green bell pepper
1 peeled, thinly sliced onion
1 8-ounce can stewed tomatoes
¼ cup orange juice
2 teaspoons vinegar
    Pinch of garlic powder
1 teaspoon oregano
½ teaspoon ground cumin

Spray a nonstick baking pan with cooking spray for no-fat cooking. Add turkey thigh, skin-side up. Bake in preheated 450-degree oven 20 to 30 minutes. Drain and discard any fat.

Combine remaining ingredients and spoon over turkey. Lower oven heat to 350 degrees. Cover pan. Bake an additional 1 hour or more, basting frequently, until turkey is tender. Then uncover and bake until sauce is thick. (Serve with rice, if desired.)

Makes five servings, under 300 calories each. (Each ½ cup fluffy rice adds about 100 calories.)

Turkey Thigh Hasenpfeffer

1 boned turkey thigh, cut into 1-inch
  cubes
⅓ cup cider vinegar
1 cup unsweetened cider or apple
  juice
½ teaspoon whole cloves
1 peeled, thinly sliced onion
3 or 4 bay leaves
2 teaspoons salt
  Pinch of ground cinnamon
5 tablespoons flour

Combine turkey cubes, vinegar, cider, cloves, on-ion, bay leaves, salt, and cinnamon in a plastic bag; set in a glass or ceramic bowl to catch any leaks. Refrigerate all day or overnight, turning occasion-ally.

Drain and reserve marinade. Shake up turkey cubes with the flour in a large paper bag. Arrange turkey skin-side down in a single layer in a shallow nonstick pan that has been sprayed with cooking spray for no-fat cooking. Put pan in preheated 450-degree oven for 20 to 25 minutes, until crisp and crusty and rendered of fat.

Pour off any fat in pan. Remove cloves and bay leaves from marinade and add liquid to the pan. Lower heat to 350 degrees. Bake until tender, about 1 hour or more, basting occasionally. (Add water, if needed.) Serve with pan juices.

Makes five servings, about 330 calories each.

One-pan Turkey Goulash

2 large boned turkey thighs, cut into
  1½-inch cubes
1 minced clove garlic (or ⅛ teaspoon
  instant garlic)
2 peeled, chopped onions
1 sliced green bell pepper
3 diced ribs celery
1 16-ounce can chopped stewed
  tomatoes
2 tablespoons Hungarian sweet
  paprika
1 bay leaf
  Salt and pepper to taste
2 teaspoons caraway seeds
½ cup dry red wine
1 cup fat-skimmed turkey or beef
  broth
2 cups water
6 ounces (dry) ruffle-edged noodles

Spray a heavy Dutch oven (or pressure cooker) with cooking spray for no-fat cooking. Add turkey cubes, skin-side down. Cook over moderate heat, uncovered, until turkey begins to brown in its own melted fat. Stir to prevent sticking. Drain and discard any melted fat. Add remaining ingredients except noodles. Cover and simmer until turkey is tender, about 1½ hours or more (or 30 minutes in a pressure cooker, according to manufacturer's directions). Skim fat, if any, from surface of broth. Add noodles to simmering liquid. Simmer, uncov-ered, until noodles are tender (about 15 minutes or more), stirring often. (Add water, if needed.)

Makes ten servings, about 365 calories each.

Philippine Turkey

2 turkey thighs or drumsticks
¾ cup (1 6-ounce can) unsweetened
    pineapple juice
2 tablespoons white vinegar
3 tablespoons soy sauce
1 tablespoon mixed pickling spices

Brown turkey under broiler, turning to brown evenly, until skin is crisp. Drain and discard any melted fat. Combine remaining ingredients and pour over turkey. Cover pan with foil and bake in preheated 350-degree oven until turkey is tender, about 1½ hours. Drain and chill. Slice and serve cold.

Makes eight to ten servings, about 285 calories each.

Turkey, Hungarian Style

2 boned, skinned turkey thighs
    (about 3 pounds), cut into 2-
    inch cubes
2 tablespoons cooking oil
1⅓ cup peeled, chopped onion
2 teaspoons paprika
1 cup water or fat-skimmed turkey
    broth
1 cup tomato juice
  Salt, pepper, and red pepper to
    taste
  optional: pinch of grated lemon
    peel
2 tablespoons flour
1 cup skim milk

Combine all ingredients except flour and milk. Cover and simmer over low heat until meat is tender, 1 hour or more. (Add more water, if needed.)

Mix flour and milk together; stir into simmering sauce. Allow to simmer 5 minutes or more, until sauce is thick.

Makes ten servings, about 330 calories each.

Turkey and Lima Stew, Lisbon Style

1 boned turkey thigh
1 cup tomato juice
2 tablespoons vinegar
1 16-ounce can undrained, chopped
    tomatoes
1 or 2 minced cloves garlic (or ¼
    teaspoon instant garlic)
1 peeled, thinly sliced onion
2 thinly sliced ribs celery
1 teaspoon mixed poultry seasoning
  optional: 1 bay leaf
1 10-ounce package frozen lima
    beans

Cut turkey meat into 2-inch cubes, leaving skin on. Spray a heavy skillet with cooking spray for no-fat frying. Add turkey, skin-side down, and brown over high heat, adding no fat. Drain and discard any melted fat.

Add tomato juice, vinegar, tomatoes, garlic, onion, celery, and seasonings. Cover and simmer over very low heat for about 1½ hours, until meat is tender. Add lima beans. Heat to simmering. Cover and simmer until tender, about 15 minutes.

Makes five servings, about 370 calories each.

Turkey à la India

1 turkey hindquarter (about 3½ pounds)
1 large, peeled, thinly sliced onion
1 minced clove garlic
1 medium unpeeled, diced, eggplant
1 seeded, thinly sliced green bell pepper
¾ cup (6-ounce can) tomato juice
  Salt to taste
1 teaspoon paprika

Place turkey hindquarter on a broiler pan and broil, turning once, until skin is crisp and well rendered of fat. Drain and discard any fat.

Place turkey in a large nonstick skillet, Dutch oven, or baking pan. Add vegetables. Combine remaining ingredients and pour over turkey. Cover and simmer (or bake at 325 degrees) until turkey is tender, 1 hour or more. Baste occasionally with sauce.

Makes ten servings, about 355 calories each.

Teriyaki Turkey Wings

2 turkey wings
⅓ cup soy sauce
¼ cup sherry
1 tablespoon minced fresh ginger root (or 1 teaspoon ground ginger)
1 large minced clove garlic
  optional: 1½ tablespoons grated orange rind

Remove wing tips and use reserve for another use. Cut each wing into 2 pieces at the joint. Place in a single layer in a shallow roasting pan. Roast, uncovered, in preheated 375-degree oven for 45 minutes, until skin is crisp. Drain and discard any melted fat. Combine remaining ingredients and pour over wings. Cover pan tightly with foil and continue baking for another 45 minutes.

Makes six servings, about 300 calories each.

Turkey Drumettes Marengo

4 turkey drumettes (first portion of wing)
1 teaspoon poultry seasoning
4 peeled, seeded, quartered ripe tomatoes
1 cup tomato juice
½ cup dry white wine
  optional: pinch of dried oregano or basil
1 cup tiny peeled onions (fresh or frozen)
1 cup sliced fresh mushrooms
  Salt and pepper to taste

Sprinkle drumettes with poultry seasoning and brown under broiler, turning to brown evenly. Combine with tomatoes, tomato juice, wine, and oregano in a heavy nonstick Dutch oven. Cover and simmer 1 hour. (Add water, if needed.) Add onions and mushrooms; simmer 5 minutes. Uncover and continue to simmer until sauce is thick. Season to taste.

Makes six servings, about 335 calories each.

Turkey Drumettes alla Cacciatore

4 turkey drumettes (first portion of
  wing)
  Salt and pepper to taste
½ cup peeled, chopped onion
1 cup sliced fresh mushrooms
1 minced clove garlic
1 seeded, sliced green bell pepper
1 cup dry white wine
2 cups chopped canned tomatoes
1 tablespoon chopped fresh parsley

Brown drumettes under broiler, turning to brown evenly. Combine with remaining ingredients in a heavy nonstick Dutch oven. Cover and simmer over low heat (or bake in preheated 375-degree oven) about 1 hour, until turkey is tender. Uncover and continue to cook until sauce is thick. (Serve with cooked spaghetti, if desired.) Spoon sauce over drumettes.

Makes six servings, about 325 calories each. (Tender-cooked spaghetti is about 155 calories per cupful.)

German Meatballs

1 sliced cubed bread (low-calorie,
  high-fiber bread may be used)
¼ cup water
2 well-beaten eggs (or 4 egg whites
  or ½ cup defrosted no-
  cholesterol substitute)
2 pounds ground turkey
½ cup peeled, minced onion
¼ cup chopped fresh parsley
  Salt to taste
¼ teaspoon pepper
2 tablespoons lemon juice
1 tablespoon Worcestershire sauce
3 cups fat-skimmed turkey broth
3 tablespoons flour
¼ cup cold water
¼ cup capers or hamburger relish

Soak bread in water. Combine with eggs, turkey, onion, parsley, salt, pepper, lemon juice, and Worcestershire sauce. Mix well and shape into 2-inch round meatballs.

Heat broth to boiling. Drop meatballs into the simmering liquid. Cook, covered, for 15 minutes. Remove turkey balls with a slotted spoon. Mix flour and cold water to form a paste and stir it into the simmering liquid. When sauce thickens, add meatballs and capers (and additional salt, pepper, and Worcestershire sauce, if desired); heat through.

Makes six dinner-size servings, about 355 calories each (340 calories each with egg whites or egg substitute).

Bavarian Turkey Meatballs

MEATBALLS:
2 pounds ground turkey
2 lightly beaten eggs (or 4 egg whites
  or ½ cup defrosted no-
  cholesterol egg substitute)
1 peeled, minced onion
  Salt and pepper to taste

Combine meatball ingredients and toss lightly to mix. Shape into 1-inch balls. Spread in a single layer on a shallow broiler pan. Broil under highest heat, turning once, until browned on both sides.

In a saucepan, combine all sauce ingredients except flour and water. Cover and simmer over low heat for 10 minutes. Combine flour and water and

SAUCE:

2 cups fat-skimmed turkey broth
2 tablespoons vinegar
¼ cup catsup
2 tablespoons golden raisins
1 bay leaf
¼ teaspoon ground ginger
 Pinch of thyme
 Pinch of ground cloves
 Salt or garlic salt to taste
 Pinch of pepper
 optional: 2 teaspoons brown gravy
   coloring
3 tablespoons flour combined with:
⅓ cup cold water

stir into sauce. Continue to simmer over low heat until liquid is gravy-thick. Add meatballs and heat through.

Makes about forty appetizer servings, under 10 calories each; or eight main-course servings, about 270 calories each (260 calories each with egg whites or egg substitute).

Turkeyburger "Cutlets" alla Parmigiana

1 pound ground turkey
1 egg (or 2 egg whites or ¼ cup
   defrosted no-cholesterol
   substitute)
¼ cup chopped fresh parsley
1 minced clove garlic (or ⅛ teaspoon
   instant garlic)
¼ teaspoon poultry seasoning
 Salt and pepper to taste
5 tablespoons Italian-seasoned bread
   crumbs
1 16-ounce can tomato sauce
½ cup fat-skimmed turkey broth
1 teaspoon dried oregano or mixed
   Italian seasoning
4 ounces shredded part-skim
   mozzarella cheese

Combine turkey, egg, parsley, garlic, poultry seasoning, salt, and pepper in a bowl and toss lightly with a fork (mixture will be very moist).

Sprinkle seasoned crumbs on a sheet of wax paper. Scoop up one-quarter of the meat mixture and drop it into the crumbs. With the palm of your hand, flatten the meat into an oval-shaped "cutlet." Press into the crumbs until lightly coated. Coat cutlet with crumbs on both sides. Arrange the four oval cutlets in a single layer on a shallow nonstick rectangular baking pan that has been sprayed with cooking spray for no-fat cooking. Put pan in preheated 450-degree oven. Add no oil. Bake 12 to 15 minutes; then turn with a spatula.

Combine tomato sauce, broth, and oregano, and pour over "cutlets." Continue baking an additional 10 minutes, until sauce is thick and bubbling. Sprinkle cutlets with shredded mozzarella and return to the oven for a minute or two, just until cheese is melted. (Serve with tender-cooked spaghetti, if desired.)

Makes four servings, about 380 calories each (370 calories each with egg white or egg substitute). (Tender-cooked spaghetti is about 155 calories per cupful.)

Turkeyburger Bourguignonne

1 pound ground turkey
1 tablespoon finely chopped fresh
    parsley
  Salt to taste
¼ teaspoon coarse pepper
2 teaspoons vegetable oil
½ cup Burgundy
½ pound sliced fresh mushrooms
⅓ cup cold water
1 tablespoon flour
¼ teaspoon sage
  Freshly chopped parsley for
    garnish

Combine the ground turkey, 1 tablespoon parsley, salt, and pepper; toss lightly. Shape into four flat patties.

Brown the patties in 1 teaspoon oil in a nonstick skillet over moderate heat, turning once. Remove to a platter.

Add second teaspoon of oil and two tablespoons wine to the skillet. Add the mushrooms. Cook, stirring, over high heat until mushrooms are lightly browned.

Stir remaining wine, water, flour, and sage together and add to the skillet. Cook, stirring, over moderate heat until sauce thickens and bubbles. Add turkey patties and simmer until heated through. Garnish with additional parsley. (Serve over rice, if desired.)

Makes four servings, about 265 calories each. (Each ½ cup fluffy rice adds about 100 calories.)

Swedish Meatballs

1 slice cubed bread (low-calorie,
    high-fiber bread may be used)
¼ cup water
1 small, peeled, minced onion
1 pound ground turkey
1 beaten egg (or 2 egg whites or ¼
    cup defrosted no-cholesterol
    substitute)
3 tablespoons ice water
  Salt to taste
¼ teaspoon pepper
⅛ teaspoon ground nutmeg
1 tablespoon butter, margarine, or
    diet margarine
2 tablespoons dry white wine
¾ cup skim milk
2 teaspoons cornstarch

Soak bread in water. Combine soaked bread, onion, turkey, egg, ice water, salt, pepper, and nutmeg. Shape into twelve meatballs.

Melt butter in a nonstick skillet. Brown the meatballs on all sides. Transfer to a hot platter.

Stir wine into the skillet and heat to bubbling. Mix milk and cornstarch together and stir into the skillet. Cook, stirring, until sauce is thick. Pour over meatballs. (Sprinkle with minced parsley, if desired.)

Makes four main-course servings, about 300 calories each (290 calories each with egg whites or egg substitute).

Breaded Swedish Turkey Patties

1 pound ground turkey
1 lightly beaten egg (or 2 egg whites or ¼-cup defrosted no-cholesterol substitute)
  Salt or garlic salt to taste
⅛ teaspoon ground nutmeg
⅛ teaspoon ground allspice
⅛ teaspoon pepper
3 tablespoons peeled, minced onion (or 1 tablespoon onion flakes)
6 tablespoons unseasoned bread crumbs
1 tablespoon salad oil

Combine all ingredients except bread crumbs and oil. Mix well. Shape into four flat patties.

Press each patty into the bread crumbs, lightly coating both sides. Heat oil in a nonstick skillet. Fry patties over moderate heat, turning once. Serve with lemon wedges.

Makes four servings, about 300 calories each (290 calories each with egg whites or egg substitute).

Turkeyburger-Green Bean Bake Italiano

1 pound ground turkey
1 cup fat-skimmed turkey broth
1 small peeled, minced onion
1 teaspoon dried oregano
1 6-ounce can tomato paste
2 16-ounce cans drained French-style green beans
1 2½-ounce jar drained sliced mushrooms
½ cup shredded part-skim mozzarella cheese

Brown ground turkey in a large nonstick skillet. Stir in broth, onion, and oregano, blend in. Add tomato paste. Cover and simmer 10 minutes. Stir in beans and mushrooms. Turn into a 2-quart casserole and top with cheese. Bake in preheated 350-degree oven 20 to 30 minutes, or until bubbly.

Makes six servings, about 225 calories each.

Greek Turkey and Eggplant Meatloaf

2 pounds ground turkey
2 eggs (or 4 egg whites or ½ cup
    defrosted no-cholesterol
    substitute)
1 8-ounce can undrained, chopped
    tomatoes
1 small trimmed, pared, shredded
    eggplant (about 1 pound)
½ cup peeled, chopped onion
1 or 2 minced cloves garlic (or ¼
    teaspoon instant garlic)
  Juice of 1 lemon
⅛ teaspoon ground nutmeg
¼ teaspoon ground cinnamon
  Salt and pepper to taste

Combine ingredients in a large bowl and mix well. Shape into loaf on a shallow baking pan. Bake in preheated 350-degree oven for 1 hour.

Makes eight servings, about 255 calories each (245 calories each with egg whites or egg substitute).

Greek Potted Turkey Balls

2 pounds ground turkey (or 1 pound
    ground turkey and 1 pound
    lean ground beef)
1 peeled, minced onion
  Salt and pepper to taste
2 eggs (or 4 egg whites or ½ cup
    defrosted no-cholesterol
    substitute)
3 slices cubed fresh bread (high-
    protein, high-fiber, or French-
    Italian bread may be used)
1 teaspoon dried mint
1 6-ounce can tomato paste
1¼ cups fat-skimmed undiluted turkey
    or beef broth (homemade or
    canned)
¼ cup dry red wine
2 tablespoons lemon juice
1 teaspoon dried oregano
¼ teaspoon nutmeg
¼ teaspoon cinnamon

Combine ground meat, onion, salt, pepper, eggs, bread, and mint. Blend well. Shape into sixteen meatballs. Brown meatballs under broiler, turning to brown evenly. Drain and discard any fat.

Stir tomato paste and broth with wine until smooth. Stir in remaining seasonings. Combine meatballs and sauce in a saucepan or skillet. Cover and simmer 20 minutes.

Makes eight servings, about 280 calories each (270 calories each with egg whites or egg substitute).

Middle Eastern Meatballs

2 pounds ground turkey (or 1 pound
    ground turkey and 1 pound
    lean fat-trimmed ground lamb
    or beef)
2 cups pared, chopped eggplant
1 cup peeled, chopped onions
4 tablespoons Italian-seasoned bread
    crumbs
2 lightly beaten eggs (or 4 egg whites
    or ½ cup defrosted no-
    cholesterol substitute)
2 tablespoons minced fresh parsley
    Salt to taste
    Pinch of pepper
1 cup tomato sauce
½ cup water
½ teaspoon prepared mustard

Combine turkey with eggplant, onion, bread crumbs, eggs, parsley, salt, and pepper. Shape into meatballs and brown under the broiler, turning frequently.

Combine tomato sauce, water, and mustard in a large skillet or saucepan. Add meatballs and cover. Simmer over low heat 15 minutes. Uncover and continue to simmer until sauce is gravy-thick (another 10 minutes).

Makes eight servings about 270 calories each with turkey; 240 calories each with turkey-meat combination (using egg whites or egg substitute subtracts 10 calories per serving).

East Indian Turkey Balls

1 pound ground turkey
1 tablespoon lemon juice
3 tablespoons peeled, chopped onion
3 minced cloves garlic (or ½
    teaspoon instant garlic)
¼ cup chopped fresh parsley (or 4
    teaspoons dried parsley)
    Salt and pepper to taste
½ teaspoon ground cinnamon
¼ teaspoon ground cloves
¼ teaspoon chili powder
3 tablespoons plain low-fat yogurt

Combine all ingredients and toss lightly to blend well. Shape into eight meatballs. Broil or barbecue 3 inches from heat source, about 8 minutes, turning to brown evenly.

Makes four servings, about 230 calories each.

Curried Apricot Sauce for Turkey or Turkey Ham

1 cup fat-skimmed turkey broth or
    water
¼ cup finely chopped dried apricots
¼ cup peeled, minced onion
¾ teaspoon curry powder
    optional: 1 tablespoon brown sugar
    Salt and pepper to taste
1 teaspoon cornstarch
¼ cup cold water

Combine all ingredients except cornstarch and water. Cover and simmer about 20 minutes, until apricots are tender. Mix cornstarch and cold water together, and stir into simmering broth, stirring until thickened. Serve over slices of hot turkey or hot turkey ham or pastrami.

Makes six servings, about 25 calories each with broth; about 20 calories each with water (brown sugar adds 8 calories per serving).

Turkey Ham and Linguini Piedmontese

½ pound (dry) linguini or thin
    spaghetti
3 tablespoons plain low-fat yogurt
2 lightly beaten eggs
1 pound diced turkey ham
6 tablespoons grated Parmesan
    cheese
2 tablespoons minced fresh parsley
    Salt and pepper to taste
⅛ teaspoon ground nutmeg

Cook linguini in salted boiling water until quite tender. Drain well; then return linguini to pot. Quickly stir in yogurt, then eggs, then turkey ham. Stir in cheese, until well mixed. Stir in parsley; add salt, pepper, and nutmeg to taste.

Makes six servings, about 310 calories each.

Linguini with Turkey Salami Sauce

2 cups fat-skimmed turkey broth
1 6-ounce can tomato paste
    optional: 1 minced clove garlic (or
        ⅛ teaspoon instant garlic)
2 teaspoons dried basil or oregano
1 pound turkey salami
6 ounces (dry) protein-enriched
    linguini or spaghetti
2 tablespoons minced fresh parsley

Combine turkey broth and tomato paste in a saucepan and stir smooth. Add garlic and basil. Cover and simmer 10 minutes.

Cut turkey salami into cubes or julienne strips. Stir into simmering sauce. Cover and simmer, until turkey salami is heated through.

Meanwhile, cook linguini according to package directions. Rinse in hot running water and drain well. Serve sauce over hot, drained pasta, garnished with parsley.

Makes four servings, about 430 calories each.

Polish Pastrami Skillet Supper

1 16-ounce can undrained tomatoes
1 tablespoon lemon juice
¾ cup (1 6-ounce can) unsweetened pineapple juice
1 6-ounce can tomato paste
½ cup peeled, sliced onions
1 head of cabbage
1 pound unsliced turkey pastrami, cut into 1½-inch cubes
    Garlic salt and pepper
1 tablespoon raisins

In a large nonstick skillet or electric frypan, combine tomatoes with lemon and pineapple juices, tomato paste, and onions. Stir well and heat to boiling. Lower heat. Cover and simmer 35 to 40 minutes.

Slice cabbage into eight equal-size wedges with the leaves still attached to the core. Add to skillet. Cover and cook an additional 8 to 10 minutes, just until tender. Add turkey pastrami, seasonings, and raisins; heat through. To serve, pour tomato sauce over cabbage wedges and pastrami.

Makes four servings, about 260 calories each.

Szechuan Stir-Fried Mushrooms and Turkey Pastrami

2 teaspoons salad oil
¼ pound thinly sliced fresh mushrooms
1 cup regular or Bloody Mary-seasoned tomato juice
1 minced clove garlic (or ⅛ teaspoon instant garlic)
1 large peeled, halved, thinly sliced onion
1 seeded, diced green bell pepper
1 pound unsliced turkey pastrami, cut into 1-inch cubes
    Soy sauce

Heat oil in a large nonstick skillet or electric frypan. Spread mushrooms in the skillet. Cook, stirring, over moderate heat until lightly browned. Stir in remaining ingredients except pastrami. Cover and simmer 5 minutes. Uncover and continue to cook, stirring frequently, until nearly all the liquid evaporates. Stir in pastrami cubes and heat through. Serve with soy sauce to taste.

Makes four servings, about 240 calories each.

Szechuan Turkey and Cashews

¾ cup (1 6-ounce can) Bloody Mary-
    seasoned tomato juice
2 tablespoons dry white wine
2 tablespoons soy sauce
4 small peeled, quartered onions
2 cups thinly sliced celery
2 cups (about 10 ounces) diced
    smoked turkey breast
1½ teaspoons cornstarch
1 cup cold water or fat-skimmed
    turkey or chicken broth
16 coarsely chopped dry-roasted
    cashews

Combine tomato juice, wine, soy sauce, onions, celery, and turkey in a nonstick skillet. Cover and cook over moderate heat, until vegetables are tender-crunchy (about 6 minutes). Combine cornstarch and cold water. Stir into skillet. Cook, stirring, until sauce thickens and clears. Then stir in cashews; heat through.

Makes four servings, about 175 calories each with water; about 180 calories each with broth.

Greek Turkey Pastitsio

3 cups (dry) protein-enriched large
    macaroni
2 beaten eggs
½ cup plain low-fat yogurt
½ cup grated Parmesan cheese
1 pound diced cooked white-meat
    turkey
1 16-ounce can tomato sauce
1 peeled, finely minced onion
½ cup chopped fresh parsley
2 teaspoons dried mint or marjoram
½ teaspoons ground cinnamon
½ teaspoon ground nutmeg

SAUCE:
1½ cups fat-skimmed turkey broth
1 13-ounce can evaporated skim milk
⅓ cup flour
    Salt or garlic salt and pepper to
    taste
2 lightly beaten eggs
½ cup grated Parmesan cheese
⅛ teaspoon nutmeg

Cook macaroni in boiling salted water until tender; drain but do not rinse. Stir eggs into hot macaroni, then stir in yogurt and Parmesan cheese.

Combine turkey, tomato sauce, onion, parsley, mint, cinnamon, and nutmeg. Mix well.

Sauce: In a saucepan, heat broth to boiling. Mix together milk, flour, salt, and pepper. Add to broth. Cook, stirring, over moderate heat until simmering. Slowly stir ¼ cup white sauce into beaten eggs. Stir egg mixture into sauce, then cook, stirring constantly, over very low heat until mixture is thick.

To assemble casserole: Layer half macaroni mixture in a nonstick baking pan. Top with turkey mixture. Add remaining macaroni mixture. Top with white sauce. Sprinkle with cheese and nutmeg. Bake, uncovered, in preheated 350-degree oven 40 to 50 minutes, until set. Cut into squares to serve.

Makes twelve servings, about 275 calories each.

TWO ▶ TURKEY IN THE OVEN

Wﾞﾞ

WITH TODAY'S versatile turkey parts and products, oven-easy meals are a breeze: inspired casseroles, family-pleasing meatloaves, fancy dinner-party dishes with self-making sauces, whole meal creations that combine turkey with vegetables and pasta, potatoes or rice. Slow-baked or quick-cooked, plain or fancy, elegant or hearty, turkey in the oven makes short work of menu-planning.

The basic techniques for roasting turkey—whole or in parts—are discussed in part three. In this section we go beyond the basics to explore some of the ways that turkeyfoods can be combined with other nutritious ingredients for easy-do meals from the oven

Turkey and Spinach Lasagna with White Sauce

8 (dry) protein-enriched lasagna noodles
2½ cups skim milk
3 tablespoons flour
Salt and pepper to taste
Pinch of ground nutmeg
3 cups well-drained cooked chopped spinach (or 2 10-ounce packages frozen spinach, cooked and well drained)
7½ ounces part-skim ricotta cheese (½ of 15-ounce container)
1½ cups diced oven-roasted turkey
3 tablespoons grated Parmesan cheese
3 tablespoons Italian-seasoned bread crumbs

Cook lasagna noodles according to package directions.

Combine milk and flour in a saucepan. Cook, stirring, over low heat until sauce is thick. Season with salt, pepper, and nutmeg. Mix half the sauce with the cooked spinach and set aside.

Pour a little of the remaining white sauce into a shallow baking dish. Add 3 or 4 cooked noodles. Top with half the spinach mixture. Add half the ricotta and a layer of turkey. Add another layer of lasagna noodles, spinach, ricotta cheese, and turkey. Pour on remaining white sauce. Sprinkle with Parmesan cheese and bread crumbs. Bake in preheated 375-degree oven 30 to 40 minutes.

Makes six servings, about 370 calories each.

Foil-baked Turkey Breast with Herbs

1 turkey breast half (about 2½ pounds)
Salt and pepper to taste
2 tablespoons grated Parmesan cheese
¼ teaspoon dried dillweed
¼ teaspoon crumbled dried basil

Note: About ⅔ cup juice collects in foil. This may be thickened slightly with cornstarch mixed with white wine or water and used as gravy.

Spread a large sheet of heavy-duty aluminum foil in a large roasting pan, shiny-side up. Set turkey on foil, skin-side up. Bake, uncovered, in preheated 450-degree oven until skin is crisp. Pour off any melted fat and discard. Sprinkle turkey with remaining ingredients. Bring up edges of foil, cover turkey, and fold over edges twice, sealing well. Lower heat to 350 degrees. Bake in foil 1½ hours, or until meat is tender. Open foil carefully, averting face to avoid steam. Slice meat and serve with juices.

Makes six servings, about 275 calories each.

Turkey Breast Adelphi

1 young turkey breast (about 2½ pounds)
2 peeled, chopped onions

Bake turkey breast skin-side up in 450-degree oven 20 to 30 minutes, until skin is crisp. Drain and discard any fat.

1 seeded, thinly sliced green bell
    pepper
1 16-ounce can chopped stewed
    tomatoes
1 cup water
2 tablespoons lemon juice
1 teaspoon dried dillweed
2 finely minced cloves garlic
1 thinly sliced lemon

Combine ingredients except lemon slices, and pour over turkey. Lower heat to 350 degrees. Cover pan and bake 1 hour or more, until turkey is tender. Uncover and bake until sauce is thick. Garnish with lemon slices.

    Makes eight servings, about 230 calories each.

Cider-baked Turkey Breast

1 turkey breast half (about 2½
    pounds)
1 cup unsweetened cider or apple
    juice
2 tablespoons soy sauce
1 tablespoon cornstarch

Bake turkey breast skin-side up, uncovered, in preheated 450-degree oven 20 to 25 minutes, until skin is crisp. Drain and discard any fat.

    Combine ¾ cup cider with soy sauce and pour over turkey. Lower heat to 350 degrees. Cover and bake 1 hour or more, basting frequently with pan liquid until turkey is tender. Skim fat from pan liquid.

    Combine cornstarch with remaining ¼ cup cider. Stir into pan. Continue to bake, uncovered, until sauce thickens. Slice turkey and spoon on sauce.

    Makes eight servings, about 220 calories each.

Tequila Turkey

1 young turkey breast portion (about
    3 pounds)
2 large peeled, sliced onions
1½ cups orange juice
½ cup tequila
1 minced clove garlic (or pinch of
    instant garlic)
2 teaspoons dried oregano
2 teaspoons cumin seeds (or ½
    teaspoon cumin powder)
  Salt and coarsely ground pepper to
    taste

Spray a nonstick roasting pan with cooking spray for no-fat cooking. Put turkey breast in the pan, skin-side up, unseasoned. Place pan in preheated 425-degree oven for 20 to 30 minutes, until skin is crisp. Drain and discard any melted fat.

    Put onion slices under turkey. Combine remaining ingredients and pour over turkey. Lower heat to 350 degrees. Cover pan and bake 1 hour or more, until turkey is tender.

    Uncover and bake until skin is crisp and liquid is reduced to a thick glaze. Baste frequently with pan liquid. (Add a tablespoon of water if the liquid evaporates too much.)

    Makes ten servings, about 235 calories each.

Turkey Breast, "Georgian Style"

1 turkey breast half (about 2½ pounds).
  Salt and pepper to taste
½ cup undiluted white grape juice
½ cup orange juice
½ cup sherry or other white wine
1 tablespoon cornstarch
½ cup cold water

Brown turkey breast skin-side up in preheated 450-degree oven until skin is crisp, about 20 minutes. Drain and discard any fat. Combine remaining ingredients except cornstarch and water, and pour over turkey. Lower heat to 350 degrees. Cover and bake, basting occasionally with pan juices, until turkey is tender, 1 hour or more. (Add water, if needed.) Skim fat from pan juices. Combine cornstarch and cold water and stir into pan. Return pan to oven and continue to bake until juices are thick. To serve, slice meat and spoon on sauce. (Garnish with seedless green grapes or sliced oranges, if desired.)

Makes eight servings, about 225 calories each.

Turkey Breast Valenciana

1 young turkey breast half (about 2½ pounds)
1 cup raw rice
1 cup orange juice
1 cup fat-skimmed turkey or chicken broth
1 peeled, minced onion
2 minced ribs celery
1 minced clove garlic (or ⅛ teaspoon instant garlic)
½ teaspoon curry powder (or more, to taste)
  Salt and pepper to taste
1 peeled, seeded, diced eating orange
1 teaspoon grated orange peel
1 seeded, diced green bell pepper

Put the turkey breast skin-side up in an oven-proof casserole. Bake, uncovered, in 450-degree oven 20 to 25 minutes, just until skin is crisp and well rendered of fat. Drain and discard any fat.

Combine rice, orange juice, broth, onion, celery, garlic, curry powder, salt, and pepper in the bottom of the casserole. Put the turkey on top, skin-side up. Lower heat to 350 degrees. Cover pan and bake 1 hour or more, until turkey is tender.

Lift turkey up and stir diced orange, orange peel, and green pepper into rice. Bake, uncovered, an additional 10 minutes.

Makes eight servings, about 265 calories each.

Turkey Tenderloin Baked in Barbecue Sauce

1 pound turkey tenderloin, cut into 4 serving pieces
2 tablespoons water

Arrange turkey in a single layer in a baking dish just large enough to hold it. Combine remaining ingredients and mix well. Spoon over turkey. Bake,

¼ cup lemon juice or vinegar
¼ cup catsup
½ teaspoon dry mustard
½ teaspoon Worcestershire sauce
3 tablespoons peeled, minced onion
    (or 1 tablespoon onion flakes)
optional: 1 minced clove garlic (or
    ⅛ teaspoon instant garlic)
Salt and pepper to taste
Few drops Tabasco sauce

uncovered, in preheated 375-degree oven 15 to 25 minutes. Baste frequently.

Makes four servings, about 160 calories each.

Turkey Creole with Mushrooms

¼ pound sliced fresh mushrooms
1 teaspoon salad oil
4 tablespoons dry white wine
1 peeled, minced onion
1 seeded, diced green bell pepper
1 small bay leaf
1 minced clove garlic (or ⅛ teaspoon
    instant garlic)
1 16-ounce can chopped stewed
    tomatoes
1 pound (4) turkey tenderloin steaks

Combine mushrooms, oil, and 2 tablespoons wine in a nonstick skillet. Cook, stirring, over high heat until mushrooms brown. Stir in remaining ingredients except turkey. Simmer, uncovered, 5 or 6 minutes. Remove bay leaf.

Arrange turkey in a single layer in a shallow nonstick baking pan. Spoon on sauce. Bake turkey, uncovered, in preheated 375-degree oven 15 to 25 minutes, basting occasionally.

Makes four servings, about 190 calories each.

Turkey Blue Ribbon

1 pound (4) turkey tenderloin steaks
4 thin slices (2 ounces) turkey ham
4 thin slices (2 ounces) Swiss cheese
2 teaspoons Dijon-style (hot)
    prepared mustard
3 tablespoons unseasoned bread
    crumbs
    Salt, pepper, and paprika to taste
2 tablespoons regular mayonnaise

Pound tenderloins flat with meat mallet. Arrange slices of turkey ham and cheese on top of tenderloins and dab lightly with mustard. Roll up with turkey ham and cheese inside. (Secure with toothpicks, if necessary.)

Mix bread crumbs, salt, pepper, and paprika. Roll turkey rolls lightly in mayonnaise and then in seasoned bread crumbs. Arrange in a single layer on a nonstick baking sheet or shallow pan that has been coated with cooking spray for no-stick baking. Bake in preheated 450-degree oven 20 minutes.

Makes four servings, under 300 calories each.

Turkey Thigh in Savory Tomato Sauce

1 young turkey thigh
Salt and pepper to taste
1 teaspoon dried savory leaves (or 1
   tablespoon fresh summer
   savory)
1 cup peeled, chopped onion
1 16-ounce can chopped tomatoes
1 cup dry white wine

Put turkey skin-side up in a shallow pan. Place pan under broiler and broil until skin is crisp and well rendered of fat, about 20 minutes. Drain and discard any fat.

Season turkey to taste. Combine remaining ingredients and pour over turkey. Cover pan with foil. Bake in preheated 300-degree oven 1½ to 2 hours, until tender. Raise heat to 425 degrees. Uncover pan and continue to bake until sauce is thick.

Makes five servings, about 310 calories each.

Turkey Thighs Supreme

2 turkey thighs (about 3 pounds)
½ cup soy sauce
1 cup water
½ cup raw brown rice
1 4-ounce can undrained mushroom
   pieces
1 peeled, minced onion
2 cups chopped celery

Combine turkey thighs, soy sauce, and water in a heavy Dutch oven. Cover and simmer on top of range or cook in 350-degree oven about 1 hour or more, just until meat is tender enough to be removed from the bone easily. Chill broth until fat rises to surface. Skim and discard fat. Chill thighs until cool enough to handle. Discard skin and bones; cut meat into bite-size pieces.

Measure 1 cup broth. (Add water, if needed.) Put fat-skimmed broth in an ovenproof casserole and stir in remaining ingredients, including meat. Cover and bake 50 to 60 minutes, until rice absorbs liquid.

Makes eight servings, about 325 calories each.

Turkey and Eggplant, Mediterranean Style

Salt and pepper to taste
1 boned turkey thigh, cut into 1-inch
   cubes
1 10¾-ounce can undiluted
   condensed tomato soup
2 tablespoons dry sherry or other
   white wine

Salt and pepper turkey cubes and place skin-side up in small roasting pan. Bake in preheated 400-degree oven about 20 minutes, until skin is brown and crispy. Pour off any fat and discard.

Combine remaining ingredients except eggplant and mushrooms, and add to pan. Cover pan with aluminum foil and place in oven. Lower heat to 325

½ cup chopped green bell pepper
optional: 1 minced clove garlic
Small bay leaf
Pinch of red cayenne pepper
1 small diced eggplant
1 cup sliced fresh mushrooms

degrees and bake until turkey is almost tender, 30 to 40 minutes. Add eggplant and mushrooms; cover and bake 30 to 35 minutes.

Makes five servings, about 345 calories each.

Slow-baked Turkey Thigh with "Cream" Sauce

3 tablespoons peeled, finely minced
    onion (or 1 tablespoon dried
    onion)
1 young turkey thigh
⅛ teaspoon poultry seasoning
    Salt or garlic salt and pepper to
    taste
2 tablespoons instant-blending flour
1 cup cold skim milk
2 tablespoons minced fresh parsley
⅛ teaspoon paprika

Put onion in a shallow nonstick casserole. Put turkey thigh on top, skin-side up. Sprinkle with seasonings. Cover and bake in preheated 325-degree oven about 1 hour 40 minutes, until turkey thigh tests tender with a fork.

Pour pan juices into a small glass and set aside, until fat rises to surface. Remove fat with a bulb-type baster.

Return turkey thigh to the oven, uncovered. Raise heat to 425 degrees and bake, uncovered, or for approximately 15 minutes or until skin is crisp.

Meanwhile, make the sauce. Heat the fat-skimmed pan juices to boiling. Combine flour and cold milk and mix well. Stir into simmering pan juices. Cook, stirring over low heat until mixture is very thick and bubbling. Season to taste. Thin, if necessary, with a little more milk. Stir in parsley and heat through. Slice the turkey thigh and top meat with sauce. Sprinkle with paprika.

Makes five servings, about 305 calories each.

Turkey Thigh Sahara with Zucchini

1 turkey thigh
1 large peeled, chopped, onion
1 8-ounce can chopped tomatoes
1 cup tomato juice
Juice of 1 lemon
¼ teaspoon ground turmeric
    optional: ¼ teaspoon ground
        cinnamon or cardamom seed
½ teaspoon dried mint (or 2
        tablespoons chopped fresh
        mint leaves)
1 teaspoon grated lemon peel
Salt and pepper to taste (if needed)
2 quartered-lengthwise medium
        zucchini, cut into 2-inch
        lengths

Brown turkey thigh under broiler; turn over to brown evenly. Drain and discard any fat. In the bottom of a heavy Dutch oven or casserole, combine all ingredients except zucchini. Put turkey thigh on top. Cover and bake at 350 degrees for 1½ hours or more, until turkey is very tender.

Uncover and put zucchini under turkey. Bake, uncovered, until liquid is reduced to a thick sauce and zucchini is tender (about 8 to 9 minutes).

Makes five servings, about 310 calories each.

Rolled Turkey Thighs with Cherries

2 turkey thighs (about 3 pounds)
Salt and pepper
¼ cup dry red wine
¼ cup red grape juice, undiluted
1 small minced onion
4 teaspoons cornstarch
½ cup liquid from cherries or water
2 cups unsweetened pitted dark
        cherries (canned or frozen)

Trim bone from turkey thighs. Season with salt and pepper, then roll and tie with skin side out. Place in a roasting pan with wine, grape juice, and onion. Bake at 350 degrees for 2 hours. Drain pan juices into a saucepan, and remove the fat with a bulb baster. Thicken the juices with a mixture of the cornstarch and the cherry juice. Add the cherries and heat thoroughly. Slice the turkey and garnish with the sauce.

Makes ten servings, about 310 calories each.

Spicy Pickled Turkey Thighs

2 skinned, boned turkey thighs
2 minced cloves garlic (or ¼ to ½ teaspoon instant garlic)
2 tablespoons mixed pickling spices

Sprinkle inside of boned thighs with half the garlic and spice; then roll up.

Spread a length of heavy-duty foil wrap (or a double layer of lightweight foil) flat and sprinkle with remaining garlic and seasonings. Add rolled up turkey thighs. Sprinkle top of the turkey with remaining seasonings.

Wrap tightly in foil. Place foil-wrapped meat in roasting pan and place in oven. Set oven control at 275 degrees. Roast 3 hours or more, until turkey is very tender but not falling apart.

Remove from oven and allow to cool still sealed in foil; then chill. To serve, remove chilled meat from broth and slice razor-thin against the grain

Makes ten servings, about 140 calories each.

Turkey Pot Roast

1 turkey hindquarter (about 3½ pounds)
Salt and pepper to taste
½ cup peeled, finely chopped onion
2 small minced cloves garlic
½ teaspoon crumbled dried basil
¼ teaspoon dried thyme
1 cup fat-skimmed turkey broth or water
3 medium pared, halved potatoes
6 medium scraped carrots, cut into chunks
1 tablespoon cornstarch
¼ cup cold water
2 tablespoons chopped fresh parsley

Place turkey hindquarter skin-side up in a nonstick Dutch oven. Salt and pepper to taste. Bake in preheated 450-degree oven 20 to 25 minutes, until skin is crisp. Drain and discard any fat.

Add onion, garlic, basil, thyme, and broth. Cover and simmer over low heat (or bake at 350 degrees) until turkey is nearly tender, about 1 hour. Add potatoes and carrots. Cover and cook until vegetables are tender, about 20 minutes.

Remove turkey and vegetables to a platter and keep warm. Skim any fat from pan juices and discard. Stir cornstarch and cold water together and stir into simmering pan juices. Cook, stirring, until sauce is thickened. Spoon over turkey and vegetables and garnish with parsley.

Makes ten servings, about 385 calories each.

Mexican Pot Roast

1 turkey hindquarter (about 3½
    pounds)
½ teaspoon poultry seasoning
1 cup fat-skimmed turkey or chicken
    broth or water
1½ cups peeled, chopped onion
1½ cups diced green and red bell
    peppers (fresh or frozen)
2 cups peeled, seeded, diced
    tomatoes (fresh or canned)
2 minced cloves garlic
    Salt and pepper to taste
¼ to ½ teaspoon chili powder (or
    more, to taste)

Arrange turkey skin-side up in a nonstick baking pan. Sprinkle with poultry seasoning. Bake in preheated 450-degree oven 20 to 25 minutes, until skin is crisp. Drain and discard any fat.

Combine remaining ingredients and spoon over turkey. Lower heat to 350 degrees. Cover and bake until tender, approximately 1 hour, basting occasionally with pan juices. (Add water, if needed.)

Makes ten servings, about 365 calories each.

Turkey Marinated in Spice Sauce

1 turkey hindquarter (about 3½
    pounds)
2 tablespoons white or red-wine
    vinegar
1 cup cider or apple juice
2 bay leaves
½ teaspoon ground cloves
¼ teaspoon ground nutmeg
¼ teaspoon ground allspice
1¼ cups fat-skimmed turkey broth

Pierce turkey with two-tine fork and marinate in mixture of all remaining ingredients several hours in refrigerator.

Remove turkey from marinade, reserving liquid. Place turkey, skin-side up, in shallow baking pan. Bake in preheated 450-degree oven 20 minutes, until skin is crisp. Drain and discard any fat.

Pour reserved marinade over turkey. Lower heat to 325 degrees. Bake, basting frequently, 1½ to 2 hours, or until tender.

Makes ten servings, about 350 calories each.

Ranch-style Turkey

2 turkey drumsticks
1 tablespoon flour
    Salt and pepper to taste
1 8-ounce can tomato sauce
1 peeled, chopped ripe tomato
1 4-ounce can mushroom stems and
    pieces

Coat drumsticks with seasoned flour. Bake in nonstick pan in preheated 400-degree oven about 40 minutes. Drain and discard any fat.

Bring other ingredients to boil in a saucepan. Pour over turkey. Bake, covered, 45 minutes, or until meat is tender. Put turkey on platter and slice. Spoon on sauce.

¼ cup peeled, minced onions
1 minced clove garlic
1 tablespoon minced parsley
2 tablespoons sliced, pitted black
   olives
   Marjoram to taste

Makes eight servings, about 210 calories each.

Hawaiian Turkey Wing Sections

2 turkey wings (about 2½ pounds)
¾ cup (1 6-ounce can) unsweetened
   pineapple juice
2 tablespoons soy sauce
⅔ cup fat-skimmed turkey broth or
   water

With a sharp knife, cut through turkey skin at the second joint. Bend each wing backward until the joint snaps; then cut skin apart to form two sections. Cut off and remove wing tips, if desired. (Wrap and freeze to use for making broth.)

Broil wing sections 30 minutes, turning once, until skin is very crisp. Drain and discard any fat.

Combine browned wing sections with remaining ingredients. Cover pan with foil. Bake in preheated 350-degree oven until wing sections are tender, about 1 hour, basting occasionally with pan liquid. Uncover and continue to bake, basting often, until pan juices evaporate into a thick glaze.

Makes six servings, about 310 calories each.

Casino Drumettes

4 turkey drumettes (first portion of
   wing) (about 2½ pounds)
½ cup creamy low-calorie French
   salad dressing
1 cup water or fat-skimmed turkey
   broth

Spray a nonstick pan with cooking spray for no-stick cooking. Add drumettes in a single layer. Bake in preheated 450-degree oven 30 minutes, turning once, until skin is crisp and well rendered of fat. Drain and discard any fat. Add remaining ingredients. Lower heat to 350 degrees. Cover pan with foil and bake 1 hour or more, until turkey is tender. Uncover and continue to bake, basting often, until pan juices evaporate into a thick glaze.

Makes six servings, 315 calories each, 320 with broth.

Spicy Drumettes

4 turkey drumettes (first portion of wing) (about 2½ pounds)
¾ cup (1 6-ounce can) Bloody Mary-seasoned tomato juice
¾ cup (1 6-ounce can) unsweetened cider or apple juice
1 tablespoon cider vinegar
1 small peeled, minced onion
Salt and pepper to taste

Spray a nonstick baking pan with cooking spray for no-stick cooking. Add drumettes in a single layer. Bake in preheated 450-degree oven 20 minutes, turning once, until skin is crisp and well rendered of fat. Drain and discard any fat. Add remaining ingredients. Cover with foil. Lower heat to 350 degrees. Bake 1 additional hour or more, until tender. Uncover and continue to bake, basting often, until pan juices evaporate to a thick glaze.

Makes six servings, about 315 calories each.

Drumettes Italiano

4 turkey drumettes (first portion of wing) (about 2½ pounds)
½ cup low-calorie Italian salad dressing
½ cup dry white wine or water
½ cup water

Spray a nonstick baking pan with cooking spray for no-stick cooking. Add drumettes in a single layer. Bake, uncovered, in preheated 450-degree oven 20 minutes, until skin is crisp and well rendered of fat. Drain and discard any fat.

Combine remaining ingredients and add to the pan. Cover and bake, basting occasionally, until tender, about 1 hour. Uncover and bake until sauce is thick.

Makes six servings, about 300 calories each.

Turkey Drumettes Baked in Spanish Sauce

4 turkey drumettes (first portion of wing) (about 2½ pounds)
½ cup water
¼ cup dry white wine or water
1 peeled, quartered onion
1 16-ounce can undrained tomatoes
optional: 1 clove garlic
3 or 4 sprigs fresh parsley
optional: 1 teaspoon dried basil
optional: 1 bay leaf
Salt and pepper to taste

Preheat oven to 450 degrees. Bake drumettes 20 minutes, until skin is crisp. Drain and discard any fat. Combine remaining ingredients in blender or food processor. With quick on-off turns, process ingredients until tomatoes are coarsely chopped. Pour sauce over wingettes and cover with foil. Lower heat to 350 degrees. Bake, uncovered, basting occasionally with sauce, until turkey is tender, about 50 to 60 minutes. (Add water to sauce, if necessary.)

Makes six servings, about 315 calories each.

Oven "Fried" Turkey Necks

5 turkey necks
3 tablespoons flour
  Salt or seasoned salt, pepper,
    paprika, and onion powder to
    taste
1 cup water

Wash necks in cold water and cut into 1-inch chunks. Dip necks into flour that has been seasoned with salt, pepper, paprika, and onion powder. Arrange in a single layer on a large shallow nonstick baking pan well coated with cooking spray for no-stick baking.

Bake in preheated 450-degree oven 20 to 25 minutes, turning once. Drain and discard any fat. Pour on water; cover pan with foil. Lower heat to 350 degrees. Bake until tender, about 45 minutes.

Makes five servings, about 390 calories each.

Italian Turkeyloaf

1 16-ounce can tomatoes
2 pounds ground turkey
2 peeled, finely chopped onions
1 seeded, minced green bell pepper
1 shredded carrot
3 eggs (or 6 egg whites or ¾ cup
    defrosted no-cholesterol
    substitute)
  optional: 1 to 2 minced cloves
    garlic
2 teaspoons salt
¼ teaspoon pepper
  optional: 1 teaspoon dried oregano
    or basil
1 cup Italian-seasoned bread crumbs

Drain tomatoes and reserve the juice. Break up tomatoes with a fork. Add remaining ingredients to tomatoes, reserving 2 or 3 tablespoons bread crumbs. Mix lightly. To shape, press mixture into a loaf pan. Then invert on a shallow roasting pan and remove loaf pan. Sprinkle top of loaf with reserved bread crumbs.

Bake in preheated 350-degree oven 1 hour 10 minutes. Baste occasionally during the last half-hour with reserved tomato juice. Serve hot or chilled.

Makes ten dinner-size servings, about 255 calories each; or sixteen sandwich-thin slices, about 160 calories each. (Subtract about 10 calories per serving if using egg whites or egg substitute.)

Easy One-step Turkeyburger Lasagna

1 pound ground turkey or turkey
    sausage
2 large peeled, minced onions
3 cups chopped Italian canned
    tomatoes
1 16-ounce can tomato sauce
1½ cups (1 12-ounce can) tomato juice
1½ teaspoons Italian seasoning or
    oregano
10 (dry) protein-enriched lasagna
    noodles
1½ cups uncreamed low-fat cottage
    cheese (pot cheese)
¾ cup shredded part-skim mozzarella
    cheese
3 tablespoons Italian-seasoned bread
    crumbs

Spray a nonstick skillet with cooking spray for no-fat frying. Spread turkey in the skillet. Brown over high heat until underside is brown; break into bite-size chunks and turn over. Brown other side. Add onions, tomatoes, sauce, juice, and Italian seasoning. Simmer 2 minutes.

Put some of the tomato-meat sauce in the bottom of an 8-inch square nonstick pan or casserole. Add a single layer of uncooked lasagna noodles, broken to fit. Add some more sauce. Add all the cottage cheese in a layer. Add remaining noodles and cover with remaining sauce. Sprinkle on the mozzarella cheese and top with bread crumbs. Double-wrap with foil and place the pan on a cookie sheet in preheated 350-degree oven. Bake 1 hour. Uncover and bake 10 to 15 minutes more.

Makes eight servings, about 360 calories each with ground turkey; 365 calories each with turkey sausage.

Easy Cheesey Turkey Loaf

1 lightly beaten egg (or 2 whites or
    ¼ cup defrosted no-cholesterol
    substitute)
½ cup skim milk
¾ cup rolled oats
1 pound ground turkey
1 peeled, chopped onion
    Salt or garlic salt to taste
½ cup shredded extra-sharp
    American or Cheddar cheese
optional: 3 tablespoons catsup

Combine ingredients except catsup, and mix lightly. Pile into a nonstick loaf pan. Spread top with catsup. Bake in preheated 350-degree oven 1 hour.

Makes six servings, about 240 calories each with eggs; about 235 calories each with egg whites or substitute (catsup adds 10 calories per serving).

Blender Turkey Loaf

1 large peeled onion
3 large ribs celery, including leaves
1 large seeded green bell pepper

Cut the vegetables in big chunks and mince in blender, adding a little cold water. Strain the vegetables and press out moisture. (Or shred the veg-

1 6-ounce can tomato paste
2 pounds ground turkey (or 1 pound
    ground turkey and 1 pound
    turkey breakfast sausage)
  Salt or garlic salt and pepper to
    taste
½ cup boiling water

etables by hand or in a food processor, using the shredding disk.)

Add two-thirds of the can of tomato paste to the turkey. Add the minced vegetables and seasonings; toss lightly, combining well. Shape the meat into a loaf in a shallow nonstick baking pan. Stir water into remaining tomato paste and pour over loaf.

Bake the loaf in preheated 350-degree oven for 1 hour, basting occasionally.

Makes eight servings, about 240 calories each (with sausage combination 245 calories per serving).

Four-meat Meatloaf

1 16-ounce can tomatoes
1 small seeded green bell pepper
1 pound ground turkey or turkey
    breakfast sausage
1 pound lean meatloaf mixture (beef-
    veal-pork)
2 eggs (or 4 egg whites or ½ cup
    defrosted no-cholesterol
    substitute)
1 coarsely shredded carrot
2 peeled, finely chopped onions
1 finely minced rib celery
½ cup fresh parsley
1 cup crushed high-protein cereal
2 teaspoons salt or garlic salt

Empty tomatoes into a strainer and reserve juice. Put drained tomatoes in a mixing bowl and break up well with fork. Slice pepper into rings; reserve a few for the top, and finely mince remaining pepper. Combine turkey and meat with tomatoes, minced pepper, and remaining ingredients. Pack into a loaf pan, then unmold into a shallow roasting pan. Arrange reserved pepper rings on top, pressing them in. Bake in preheated 350-degree oven, basting frequently with reserved tomato juice, 1 hour 10 minutes. Slice to serve.

Makes ten servings, about 200 calories each; with egg whites or substitute, about 190 calories each.

Italian Mock Veal Loaf

1 pound lean ground beef round
1 pound ground turkey
¾ cup Italian-seasoned bread crumbs
2 lightly beaten eggs (or 4 egg whites or ½ cup defrosted no-cholesterol substitute)
1 6-ounce can tomato paste
½ cup chopped onion (fresh or frozen)
½ cup chopped green bell pepper (fresh or frozen)
1 large minced clove garlic (or ¼ teaspoon instant garlic)
½ teaspoon dried oregano or mixed Italian seasoning (or to taste)
Dash of hot pepper or Tabasco sauce
Salt and pepper to taste

Note: If using plain bread crumbs, increase oregano to 1 teaspoon.

Combine ingredients and toss lightly. Pile into a nonstick roasting pan and shape gently into a loaf. Bake in a 350-degree oven 1 hour or more, until a meat thermometer reads 185 degrees. Remove to a platter. Deglaze the pan by adding a few tablespoons of boiling water to the pan and scraping well. Pour gravy over the meatloaf.

Makes ten servings, about 210 calories each (200 calories each with egg whites or substitute).

Olive and Pimiento Turkey Loaf

8 slices dry or toasted bread (high-fiber bread may be used)
2 pounds ground turkey
2 beaten eggs (or 4 egg whites or ½ cup defrosted no-cholesterol substitute)
20 stuffed green olives
2 seeded, finely chopped red or green bell peppers
2 peeled, finely chopped onions
optional: 1 minced clove garlic (or ⅛ teaspoon instant garlic)
¼ cup chopped fresh parsley
Salt and pepper to taste
½ teaspoon cinnamon
¼ teaspoon nutmeg

Moisten bread in water, then squeeze out well. Combine with remaining ingredients, mixing lightly. Pack meat into a loaf pan to shape. Then invert on a shallow baking pan; remove loaf pan.

Bake loaf, uncovered, in preheated 350-degree oven 1¼ hours, or until a meat thermometer inserted in the center reads 185 degrees. Serve hot or cold.

Makes ten slices, about 255 calories each (245 calories each with egg whites or egg substitute).

Savory Turkey Loaf

2 eggs (or 4 egg whites or ½ cup
   defrosted no-cholesterol
   substitute)
  Salt and pepper to taste
1 cup peeled, chopped onion
1 tablespoon Worcestershire sauce
1 tablespoon dry mustard
2 cups (1 16-ounce can) tomato
   sauce
2 pounds ground turkey
3 tablespoons cider vinegar
¾ cup (1 6-ounce can) unsweetened
   apple juice or cider

Mix eggs, salt, pepper, onion, Worcestershire sauce, 1 teaspoon dry mustard, and ¾ cup tomato sauce with ground turkey. On shallow baking pan shape mixture into a loaf. Combine remaining tomato sauce, vinegar, remaining dry mustard, and apple juice; pour over the meat loaf. Bake, uncovered, at 350 degrees 1 hour. Slice and serve.

Makes eight servings, about 265 calories each (255 calories each with egg whites or egg substitute).

Turkey Pickle and Pimiento Loaf

8 slices dry or toasted bread (high-
   fiber bread may be used)
2 pounds ground turkey
2 beaten eggs (or 4 egg whites or ½
   cup defrosted no-cholesterol
   substitute)
1 large seeded, chopped red bell
   pepper
2 peeled, chopped onions
1 small chopped pickle (or ½ cup dill
   pickle relish)
1 teaspoon dried oregano
  Salt or garlic salt to taste
  Pinch of red cayenne pepper or
   dash of hot pepper sauce

Moisten bread in water, then squeeze out. Combine with remaining ingredients. Pack in a loaf pan to shape. Then invert on a shallow baking pan; remove loaf pan. Bake loaf, uncovered, in preheated 350-degree oven for 1¼ hours, or until a meat thermometer inserted in the center reads 185 degrees. Serve hot or cold.

Makes ten slices, about 235 calories each (225 calories each with egg whites or egg substitute).

Cheddar-baked Zucchini and Turkey Ham

3 medium sliced zucchini (or 2 10-ounce packages, defrosted)
3 ounces diced extra-sharp Cheddar cheese broken up
1 16-ounce can chopped tomatoes
1 pound cubed turkey ham
3 tablespoons Italian-seasoned bread crumbs

Put a layer of zucchini in the bottom of a casserole or baking dish. Add layers of cheese, tomatoes, and turkey ham. Continue layering zucchini, cheese, tomatoes and turkey ham; then sprinkle with crumbs. Bake in preheated 350-degree oven 20 to 30 minutes until tender, brown, and bubbly.

Makes six servings, about 205 calories each.

Curried Ham Rolls

1 cup cooked rice
½ cup minced celery
¼ cup peeled, minced onion
6 tablespoons raisins
6 tablespoons drained, juice-packed crushed pineapple
2 tablespoons regular or low-calorie mayonnaise
¾ pound (12 slices) turkey ham

SAUCE:
2 tablespoons flour
¾ cup fat-skimmed turkey or chicken broth
¾ cup skim milk
1½ teaspoons curry powder
Pinch of ground ginger
Salt and pepper to taste

Combine cooked rice, celery, onion, raisins, pineapple, and enough mayonnaise to moisten the mixture. Fill each ham slice with 3½ tablespoons rice mixture. Roll firmly and arrange in 8-inch nonstick square pan with seam sides down.

In a saucepan cook and stir sauce ingredients until bubbling. Pour sauce over ham rolls. Cover pan with foil and bake in preheated 350-degree oven 30 minutes.

Makes six servings, about 230 calories each. (Low-calorie mayonnaise reduces each serving by 25 calories.)

Turkey Ham Rolls with "Sour Cream" Sauce

1 pound (16 slices) turkey ham
2 10-ounce packages defrosted French-cut green beans or asparagus spears, or 1 package of each

Fill each ham slice with a little of the defrosted uncooked vegetable. Roll up and place seam-side down in a nonstick baking pan. (Alternate rolls if using both vegetables.)

Stir remaining ingredients together and pour

1 cup low-fat sour dressing
Pinch of garlic powder
Salt to taste
Dash of paprika

over rolls. Cover pan with foil and bake in preheated 350-degree oven 30 minutes.

Makes eight servings, about 150 calories each.

Turkey Salami and Ziti Al Forno

8 ounces (dry) ziti or elbow
   macaroni
1 8-ounce can chopped, undrained
   stewed tomatoes
1 8-ounce can tomato sauce
1 peeled, finely chopped onion
   optional: 1 minced clove garlic (or
   ⅛ teaspoon instant garlic)
½ teaspoon dried oregano
   Salt and pepper to taste
1 pound diced turkey salami
2 ounces diced aged sharp Provolone
   or other sharp cheese
2 tablespoons Italian-seasoned bread
   crumbs

Cook ziti in salted water until tender-firm; then drain. Combine with all ingredients except bread crumbs. Spoon into a casserole and sprinkle with crumbs. Bake in preheated 400-degree oven 20 minutes.

Makes six main-course servings, about 355 calories each.

THREE ▶ SKILLET-EASY TURKEY DISHES

THE SKILLET—or frying pan—is synonymous with speedy meals. And with today's turkey, what a great combination! Turkey-in-the-skillet dinners can be table-ready in next to no time, with little or no fat needed. The frying pan can be a lot more versatile than its name indicates. So, even if you *are* calorie-conscious, you don't need to relegate your skillet or electric frypan to the top shelf. This chapter shows you how short-order meals with little fat and few calories are possible in your skillet, with today's turkey parts and products. If you want to cut down on fat and calories, be sure to use a skillet or frying pan with a nonstick finish.

Turkey-Cashew Curry

1 small peeled, chopped onion
1 cup fat-skimmed turkey broth
1 cup plain low-fat yogurt
3 tablespoons all-purpose flour
2 teaspoons curry powder (or more, to taste)
  Salt and pepper to taste
2 cups (about 10 ounces) diced cooked turkey
2 cups cooked white rice
3 tablespoons coarsely chopped dry-roasted cashews
  Minced fresh parsley

Combine onion with ½ cup broth in a saucepan. Cover and simmer 2 minutes. Stir remaining broth, yogurt, flour, curry powder, salt, and pepper together; then stir into saucepan. Cook and stir until sauce simmers and thickens. Add diced turkey and gently heat through. Serve over rice, garnished with cashews and chopped parsley. (Season with soy sauce, if desired.)

Makes four servings, about 355 calories each.

Speedy Skillet Chow Mein

1 cup peeled, chopped onion (fresh or frozen)
1¼ cups fat-skimmed undiluted turkey or chicken broth (homemade or canned)
1 16-ounce can rinsed, drained Chinese vegetables
2 cups diced cooked turkey
2 tablespoons soy sauce
1 tablespoon cornstarch

Simmer onions in broth, uncovered, for 3 minutes. Add drained vegetables and turkey; heat to boiling. Combine soy sauce and cornstarch and stir into saucepan. Reduce heat to simmering, and cook until thickened. (Serve over rice, if desired.)

Makes four servings, 190 calories each. (1 cup fluffy rice adds about 200 calories.)

Turkey Skillet Stroganoff

2 teaspoons salad oil
1 pound raw turkey breast slices
2 tablespoons dry sherry or other white wine
1 small peeled, minced onion
¼ pound thinly sliced fresh mushrooms
1 tablespoon flour
⅔ cup skim milk
⅛ teaspoon ground nutmeg
  Salt and pepper to taste
  optional: fresh parsley, paprika

Spray a large nonstick skillet with cooking spray for no-stick frying. Add oil and turkey slices. Brown turkey quickly over high heat. Remove to a platter.

Combine wine, onion, and mushrooms in the skillet over high heat. Cook, stirring to prevent sticking.

Combine flour and skim milk. Stir into skillet. Cook, stirring constantly, until thickened. Season to taste. Add turkey slices. Simmer 2 or 3 minutes over low heat, stirring frequently. Sprinkle with parsley and paprika before serving.

Makes four servings, about 190 calories each.

Stir-fried Turkey and Broccoli with Almonds

4 tablespoons slivered almonds
1 teaspoon salad oil
½ pound turkey breast slices, cut into ½-inch strips
1 large peeled, halved, thinly sliced Spanish onion
1 minced clove garlic
¾ cup fat-skimmed turkey or chicken broth
1 small seeded, sliced red or green bell pepper
½ pound cut up fresh broccoli (or 1 10-ounce package defrosted diagonally sliced broccoli spears)
½ cup dry white wine
optional: ½ teaspoon MSG
½ teaspoon cornstarch
2 tablespoons soy sauce

Spread almonds on a large nonstick skillet over high heat. Shake the skillet gently, until almonds are browned (be careful they don't burn). Remove almonds and set aside. Combine oil and turkey in the same skillet. Sear turkey quickly. Remove to a plate and set aside.

Combine onion, garlic, and ¼ cup broth in the skillet over high heat. Cook and stir until broth evaporates and onions are browned lightly.

Add to the skillet the pepper, broccoli, wine, and MSG. Stir in remaining ½ cup broth. Cook over medium heat, stirring occasionally, about 5 to 8 minutes, just until vegetables are tender-crisp.

Combine cornstarch with soy sauce and stir into skillet, until pan liquid simmers and thickens and vegetables are coated. Stir in turkey strips; cook, stirring, until heated through. Sprinkle with almonds.

Makes two servings, about 370 calories each. (Recipe may be doubled to serve four.)

Turkey Chinatown

1 pound sliced turkey breast
5 tablespoons soy sauce
1 tablespoon salad oil
2 medium green bell peppers, sliced in thin strips
1 minced clove garlic
2½ cups sliced fresh mushrooms
2 cups fat-skimmed turkey, chicken, or beef broth
2 8-ounce cans drained, sliced water chestnuts
½ teaspoon ground ginger
4 teaspoons cornstarch
¼ cup cold water
6 tablespoons dry-roasted cashews

Slice turkey horizontally in ¼-inch strips. Combine with 3 tablespoons soy sauce and let stand while vegetables are being prepared.

Heat oil in a heavy nonstick skillet. Add green peppers, garlic, and mushrooms. Stir-fry for 3 minutes. Add broth, water chestnuts, and turkey mixture. Add 2 remaining tablespoons soy sauce and ginger. Mix well and cook until turkey slices turn from pink to white (about 15 minutes).

Combine cornstarch with cold water and stir into skillet. Cook, stirring, until sauce is thick. Stir in cashews.

Makes six servings, about 265 calories each.

Smothered Turkey Tidbits

½ pound sliced fresh mushrooms
1 large peeled, halved, thinly sliced
  onion
½ cup dry sherry
1½ cups fat-skimmed turkey or
  chicken broth (homemade or
  canned)
1 pound turkey tenderloin, cut into
  1-inch cubes

Spray a large nonstick skillet or electric frypan with cooking spray for no-stick cooking. Combine all ingredients in skillet. Cover and simmer, stirring frequently, for 5 to 6 minutes, until onions are tender-crisp. Uncover.

Cook, stirring constantly, until nearly all the liquid has evaporated, 3 to 4 minutes.

Makes four servings, about 175 calories each.

Stir-fried Turkey Tenderloins

1 tablespoon salad oil
1 pound turkey tenderloin, cut into
  1-inch cubes
1 peeled, halved, thinly sliced onion
1 cup sliced fresh mushrooms
1 8-ounce can drained, sliced water
  chestnuts
1 seeded, diced green bell pepper
1 cup diagonally sliced celery
¾ cup fat-skimmed turkey or chicken
  broth
  Soy sauce to taste

Heat oil in a large nonstick skillet or electric frypan. Add turkey cubes and stir-fry 2 minutes. Add onion and mushrooms. Stir-fry 1 minute. Add remaining ingredients. Lower heat. Simmer, uncovered, stirring frequently, until broth evaporates, about 10 minutes.

Makes four servings, about 245 calories each.

Curried Turkey with Onions

1½ pounds turkey breast steaks
½ cup plain low-fat yogurt
4 tablespoons lemon juice
2 teaspoons curry powder
⅛ teaspoon pumpkin pie spice
  Salt and pepper to taste
2 tablespoons butter
1 tablespoon water
1 large peeled, thinly sliced onion

Cut turkey steaks into 3-inch strips. Combine yogurt, lemon juice, curry powder, pumpkin pie spice, salt, and pepper. Marinate turkey strips in this mixture for several hours in the refrigerator.

Melt butter in a nonstick skillet. Wipe marinade off meat with a spoon, reserving the marinade. Fry turkey strips over high heat for 3 minutes, turning frequently. Remove to a platter.

Add the water and onion to skillet. Cook, stirring, over high heat until liquid evaporates and onion is golden and tender-crisp. Put onion on top of the turkey.

Put remaining yogurt marinade in skillet. Cook, stirring and scraping the pan well, until mixture simmers. Return turkey and onions to skillet over medium heat and stir, coating with sauce. Serve immediately.

Makes six servings, about 185 calories each.

Turkey Primrose

2 teaspoons salad oil
1 pound turkey breast tenderloin, cut
  into 1½-inch cubes
¾ cup (1 6-ounce can) tomato juice
1 4-ounce can drained, sliced water
  chestnuts
1 4-ounce can drained sliced
  mushrooms
1 peeled, halved, thinly sliced onion
1 cup diagonally sliced celery
2 tablespoons soy sauce
½ head iceberg lettuce, cut into 2-
  inch cubes

Heat oil in nonstick skillet over high heat. Add turkey chunks and brown quickly. Stir in all remaining ingredients except lettuce. Cover and simmer over low heat 5 minutes. Uncover. Simmer until sauce is thick. Stir in lettuce, and heat through.

Makes four servings, about 260 calories each.

Turkey and Zucchini Parmesan

1 pound turkey breast tenderloin
  steaks
1 tablespoon olive oil

Cut turkey steak into 1½-inch cubes. Heat oil in a nonstick skillet. Brown turkey cubes over moderate heat. Add remaining ingredients except cheese.

2 sliced zucchini
1 large peeled onion, sliced into rings
1 cup tomato juice
½ teaspoon dried oregano
   optional: 1 minced clove garlic (or
      ⅛ teaspoon instant garlic)
3 tablespoons grated Parmesan
   cheese

Cover and simmer about 3 minutes, until onion rings are tender but still crunchy. Uncover and continue to cook over moderate heat until turkey and vegetables are coated with sauce. Sprinkle with cheese.

Makes four servings, about 220 calories each.

Turkey and Zucchini, Japanese Style

1 pound turkey breast tenderloin
   steaks
2 medium zucchini
1 tablespoon salad oil
4 peeled, quartered onions
1 tablespoon soy sauce
3 tablespoons sherry
1 cup tomato juice
   optional: ¼ teaspoon MSG

Slice turkey into 1½-inch cubes. Cut squash into quarters lengthwise, then into 3-inch lengths. Heat oil in nonstick skillet. Brown turkey cubes over moderate heat. Add remaining ingredients. Cover and simmer 3 minutes. Uncover; cook, stirring, until most of the liquid evaporates and meat and vegetables are coated with a thick sauce. Vegetables should be crunchy.

Makes four servings, about 230 calories each.

One-pan Turkey au Vin Rouge

2 teaspoons salad oil
1 pound turkey tenderloin steaks, cut
   into 1-inch cubes
2 cups dry red wine
2 cups water
1 cup fat-skimmed turkey or chicken
   broth
2 peeled, halved, sliced onions
1 bay leaf
¼ teaspoon poultry seasoning
   Salt and pepper to taste
4 ounces (dry) wide noodles
¼ pound turkey ham, cut into ½-inch
   cubes
2 tablespoons chopped fresh parsley

Spray a large nonstick pot or Dutch oven with cooking spray for no-stick cooking. Heat the oil. Add turkey tenderloin cubes. Brown slowly over moderate heat, stirring to prevent sticking.

Combine wine, water, broth, onions, bay leaf, and seasonings and add to pot.

Heat to boiling. Stir in the noodles, a few at a time. Cover and simmer 12 to 15 minutes, stirring occasionally. Uncover and continue to simmer until all of the liquid is absorbed by the noodles. Stir in turkey ham and heat through. Sprinkle with parsley.

Makes four servings, about 345 calories each.

Turkey Supreme with Mushrooms

1 turkey breast tenderloin (about 1 pound)
1 tablespoon butter, margarine, or diet margarine
¾ cup white wine
½ pound small whole fresh mushrooms
2 tablespoons peeled, minced onion
Salt and pepper to taste
Pinch of nutmeg
1 teaspoon cornstarch
1 tablespoon fresh minced parsley

Cut turkey into 1½-inch cubes. Combine butter with 1 tablespoon wine in a large nonstick skillet. Add turkey, mushrooms, and onion. Cook over high heat, uncovered, until liquid evaporates. Cook, stirring, to brown lightly. Add ½ cup wine, salt, pepper, and nutmeg. Lower heat. Cover and simmer 10 minutes.

Combine remaining 2 tablespoons wine with cornstarch and stir into simmering skillet until sauce thickens. Serve sprinkled with parsley.

Makes four servings, about 175 calories each (165 with diet margarine).

Turkey Waikiki

1 16-ounce can undrained, juice-packed pineapple tidbits
1 cup fat-skimmed turkey broth
2 peeled, onions cut in chunks
2 seeded, diced, red or green bell peppers (or 1 of each)
1 pound turkey fillets, cut into 1-inch cubes
2 tablespoons soy sauce (or to taste)

Spray a large nonstick skillet or electric frypan with cooking spray for no-stick cooking. Drain pineapple juice into skillet, reserving the tidbits. Add remaining ingredients. Cover and simmer 5 minutes, stirring frequently. Add the pineapple. Uncover and raise heat. Cook, stirring, until most of the liquid has evaporated and the turkey is tender (3 to 4 minutes). Add soy sauce to taste.

Makes four servings, about 235 calories each.

Potted Turkey Meatballs

1 pound lean ground turkey
2 teaspoons salad oil
1 small peeled, minced onion
1 cup tomato juice
⅓ cup unsweetened applesauce
1 teaspoon cider vinegar

Shape ground turkey into eight meatballs.

Coat a nonstick skillet lightly with oil. Brown the meatballs slowly over moderate heat, turning carefully. Add remaining ingredients. Simmer, uncovered, for 15 minutes, until most of the liquid evaporates into a thick sauce.

Makes four servings, about 275 calories each.

Turkey Piccadillo

1 pound ground turkey
2 peeled, halved, thinly sliced onions
1 thinly sliced rib celery
2 tablespoons sherry
1½ tablespoons lemon juice
1 cup tomato juice
¼ cup thinly sliced stuffed green
   olives
¼ cup olive juice (from jar)
4 tablespoons golden raisins
1 or 2 chopped cloves garlic (or ¼
   teaspoon instant garlic)
½ teaspoon cumin seeds (or ⅛
   teaspoon ground cumin)
Salt and pepper to taste

Spray a nonstick skillet with cooking spray for no-stick cooking. Spread turkey in skillet. Brown turkey over moderate heat. Break up into chunks. Drain and discard any fat. Add remaining ingredients. Simmer, uncovered, until most of the liquid has evaporated, stirring frequently.

Makes four servings, about 285 calories each.

Trader's Turkeyburger Skillet

1 pound ground turkey
2 peeled, halved, thinly sliced onions
1 thinly sliced rib celery
1½ tablespoons soy sauce
   optional: 1 small minced clove
      garlic
2 teaspoons curry power (or to taste)
¾ cup (1 6-ounce can) tomato juice
½ cup undrained, juice-packed
   crushed pineapple
   optional: 1 unpeeled, diced red
      apple

Brown turkey and break into chunks as directed in recipe for Turkey Piccadillo above. Drain and discard fat. Add all remaining ingredients except diced apple. Simmer uncovered, stirring frequently, until nearly all liquid is absorbed. Stir in apples last and heat through.

Makes four servings, about 270 calories each without apple; apples add about 20 calories per serving.

Turkeyburger Puchero

1 pound ground turkey
¾ cup fat-skimmed turkey broth
¼ cup dry white wine
2 peeled, seeded, chopped ripe
   tomatoes
2 peeled, halved, thinly sliced onions
3 tablespoons golden raisins
4 dried apricot halves
1 small bay leaf
¼ teaspoon poultry seasoning
2 unpeeled, diced red apples (or 2
   unpeeled, diced, fresh pears or
   1 of each)
Salt and pepper to taste

Spread the ground turkey in a large nonstick skillet or electric frypan over high heat, with no fat added. Brown the underside of the meat. Then break up into bite-size chunks, turn, and brown other side. Pour off and discard any fat.

Add broth, wine, tomatoes, onions, raisins, apricots, bay leaf, and poultry seasoning. Simmer uncovered, stirring frequently, until nearly all the liquid is evaporated. Stir in apples and/or pears and salt and pepper to taste. Continue to cook, stirring, until fresh fruit is tender but not soft.

Makes four servings, about 330 calories each.

Turkey-Lima Bean Chili

1 pound ground turkey or turkey
   breakfast sausage
1 peeled, chopped onion
2 peeled, seeded, chopped ripe
   tomatoes (or 1 8-ounce can)
1 seeded, sliced green bell pepper
1 minced rib celery
1 10-ounce package frozen lima
   beans
1 cup tomato juice
2 teaspoons chili powder (or to taste)
Garlic salt and pepper to taste

Spread the ground turkey in a nonstick skillet sprayed with cooking spray for no-fat frying. Brown over moderate heat; then break into chunks. Turn to brown evenly. Drain and discard any fat. Add remaining ingredients. Cover and simmer 15 minutes, until lima beans are tender. Uncover and continue to cook until most of the liquid evaporates.

Makes four servings, about 325 calories each with ground turkey; 335 calories each with turkey breakfast sausage.

Turkey Stuffed Peppers

FILLING:
1 pound ground turkey or turkey
   breakfast sausage
1 16-ounce can undrained Italian
   tomatoes
1 cup fat-skimmed turkey or chicken
   broth
⅓ cup raw rice
1 cup chopped onion
1 teaspoon garlic salt

Spray a large nonstick skillet with cooking spray for no-fat frying. Spread ground turkey in skillet and cook over high heat until underside is browned. Break into chunks and turn over. Continue cooking until meat is well browned. (Drain and discard any fat that accumulates in the pan.)

Add the undrained tomatoes and break up well with a fork. Add ⅓ cup broth. Stir in rice, onion, and seasonings. Cover and simmer, stirring occasionally, until rice is tender, about 15 minutes.

optional: dash of Tabasco sauce
¼ teaspoon poultry seasoning
1½ teaspoons dried basil
6 green bell peppers
1 8-ounce can tomato sauce
3 tablespoons Italian-seasoned breadcrumbs
1 tablespoon grated Parmesan cheese

Meanwhile, slice tops off peppers; remove seeds and inner membranes.

When filling is cooked, spoon into peppers. Stand filled peppers upright in a baking dish. Combine tomato sauce and remaining ⅔ cup broth, and pour over peppers. Combine bread crumbs and Parmesan cheese and sprinkle over the filling. Bake, uncovered, in preheated 350-degree oven 25 to 30 minutes, basting occasionally.

Makes six servings, under 260 calories each.

Spicy Italian Turkey Sausage Patties

1 pound turkey breakfast sausage
¼ teaspoon pumpkin pie spice (or pinch of cinnamon, nutmeg, ginger, and cloves)
1 teaspoon garlic salt
Pinch of red pepper flakes
2 tablespoons dry red wine

Combine and shape into eight patties. Broil or panfry in a nonstick skillet with no fat added. (Serve with tomato sauce, if desired.)

Makes eight patties, about 110 calories each.

Turkey Ham and Cheese with Spinach and Noodles

8 ounces creamed, large curd cottage cheese
8 ounces (dry) egg noodles or green spinach noodles
1 tablespoon olive or salad oil
1 minced clove gralic
¾ pound washed, trimmed, fresh spinach, torn in bite-size pieces (or 1 10-ounce package defrosted chopped spinach, drained)
1 pound turkey ham or salami, cut into 1-inch cubes
2 tablespoons grated Parmesan cheese
¼ cup chopped fresh parsley
1 tablespoon fresh basil or oregano (or 1 teaspoon dried)
Salt and coarsely ground pepper to taste

Remove cottage cheese from refrigerator ahead of time to reach room temperature. Cook noodles in boiling salted water, according to package directions. Combine oil and garlic in a large nonstick skillet. Sauté garlic over moderate heat until golden; then add spinach and turkey ham. Cook, stirring, over low flame just until heated through.

Drain noodles and rinse under hot water. Combine hot drained noodles, spinach, garlic, turkey ham mixture, and cottage cheese in skillet over very low heat. Add remaining ingredients and toss lightly to combine. Serve immediately.

Makes six servings, about 340 calories each with turkey ham; 380 calories each with turkey salami.

Speedy Hawaiian Turkey Ham and Vegetable Skillet

¾ cup (1 6-ounce can) unsweetened
    pineapple juice
1 10-ounce package frozen cut
    broccoli
½ cup peeled, chopped onion (fresh
    or defrosted)
½ cup chopped bell pepper
    (preferably red or red and
    green, fresh or frozen)
2 tablespoons soy sauce
2 teaspoons cornstarch
1 pound unsliced turkey ham, cut
    into 1-inch cubes

Combine pineapple juice, frozen broccoli, onion, and pepper. Cover and cook 3 minutes. Uncover and stir vegetables well. Cook until tender but crisp. Combine soy sauce and cornstarch and stir into simmering skillet until mixture thickens slightly. Add ham and heat through.

Makes four servings, about 220 calories each.

Green Beans with Turkey Ham

2 ounces (4 slices) diced turkey ham
10 ounces green beans (fresh or partly
    defrosted)
¼ cup seeded, diced red or green bell
    pepper
3 tablespoons low-calorie Italian
    salad dressing
¼ cup water

Brown turkey ham lightly in a nonstick saucepan. Remove and set aside.

Combine remaining ingredients in the saucepan. Cover and cook 3 minutes. Uncover and simmer until most of the liquid has evaporated. Add diced turkey ham. Serve hot or cold.

Makes four servings, about 45 calories each.

Turkey Franks 'n' Sauerkraut

4 turkey frankfurters, diagonally
    sliced
2 cups fresh or canned sauerkraut
2 large onions, minced
6 ounce (¾ cup) can unsweetened
    apple juice or cider
2 teaspoons caraway seeds
2 unpeeled red apples, cored and
    thinly sliced

Spray a nonstick skillet or electric frying pan with cooking spray for no-fat frying. Brown the franks quickly. Remove and set aside.

Drain the sauerkraut, then add to the skillet, along with the minced onion, apple juice, and caraway seeds.

Cover tightly and simmer over low heat until onions are tender, about 20 minutes. Uncover, stir in sliced apple and franks. Heat through.

Makes four servings, about 160 calories each.

Smoked Turkey Chop Suey

¾ cup fat-skimmed turkey broth
1 16-ounce bag frozen mixed Chinese
    vegetables (or 1 16-ounce can,
    drained)
½ cup thinly sliced celery
½ cup peeled, thinly sliced onions
2 cups diced cooked smoked turkey
    (from smoked breast,
    wingettes, or drumsticks)
2 tablespoons sherry
6 tablespoons water
2 tablespoons soy sauce
1 tablespoon cornstarch

Combine broth, Chinese vegetables, celery, and onions in nonstick skillet. Cover and simmer until tender-crisp. Add smoked turkey; cook and stir until heated through. Combine wine, water, soy sauce, and cornstarch and stir into skillet; cook, stirring, until mixture bubbles and thickens.

Makes four servings, about 455 calories each.

Italian Green Beans and Turkey Bologna

1 8-ounce can chopped tomatoes
1 peeled, finely chopped onion
¼ cup water or fat-skimmed turkey
    broth
    Garlic salt and pepper to taste
½ teaspoon dried oregano or pizza
    seasoning
¾ pound fresh Italian green beans (or
    1 10-ounce package, frozen)
1 pound turkey bologna, cut into ½-
    inch cubes

Combine all ingredients except beans and bologna. Cover and simmer 10 minutes.

Meanwhile, wash and tip fresh green beans. (If using frozen beans, allow to defrost partially.) Add beans to tomato mixture. Simmer uncovered, stirring often, until beans are tender and most of the liquid has evaporated into a thick sauce. Stir in bologna and heat through.

Makes six servings, about 185 calories each.

Sweet 'n' Sour Cabbage and Turkey Bologna

2 cups fat-skimmed turkey broth (or
    2 cups boiling water and 2
    cubes or envelopes beef
    bouillon)
1 tablespoon red-wine vinegar
1 6-ounce can tomato paste
1 peeled, chopped onion
½ cup undrained, unsweetened
    canned crushed pineapple
1 quartered medium head cabbage
1 pound turkey bologna, cut into
    julienne strips

Heat broth to boiling in a large pot. (If using bouillon, add to water and stir until dissolved.) Stir in wine vinegar and tomato paste until smooth. Add onion and pineapple; cover and simmer 6 minutes, until onions are tender. Add cabbage wedges. Cover and cook about 10 minutes, until cabbage is tender but still crisp and green and sauce is thick. Add turkey bologna and heat through. To serve, arrange cabbage on individual plates and spoon on sauce.

Makes four servings, about 315 calories each.

Skillet Turkey Salami Ratatouille

1 small pared, diced eggplant
1 small unpeeled, diced zucchini
1 peeled, halved, thinly sliced onion
1 16-ounce can undrained, chopped tomatoes
½ cup fat-skimmed turkey broth or water
Salt and pepper to taste
¼ teaspoon dried basil or oregano
1 pound unsliced turkey salami or bologna, cut into 1-inch cubes

Spray a large nonstick skillet or electric frypan with cooking spray for no-stick cooking. Combine all ingredients except turkey. Cover and simmer 10 minutes, stirring frequently, until vegetables are tender but still crisp.

Uncover and add turkey cubes. Cook uncovered, stirring, until nearly all the liquid is evaporated.

Makes four servings, about 285 calories each.

Sautéed Zucchini and Turkey Salami

2 medium thinly sliced zucchini
1 teaspoon olive oil
1 tablespoon water
Salt and pepper to taste
optional: ¼ teaspoon dried oregano or mixed Italian seasoning
1 pound unsliced turkey salami, cut into 1-inch cubes

Combine all ingredients in a large nonstick skillet or electric frypan, with zucchini slices and turkey salami arranged in a single layer. Raise heat to high and cook undisturbed until all the moisture evaporates and zucchini slices begin to "fry" in the remaining oil. Turn to brown other side lightly. (Zucchini should be crisp.)

Makes four servings, about 240 calories each.

Greek Peppers and Pastrami

4 green seeded, sliced bell peppers
1 16-ounce can chopped tomatoes
Salt and pepper to taste
⅛ teaspoon dillweed
¼ teaspoon dried oregano
¼ teaspoon poultry seasoning
1 pound diced turkey pastrami

Combine ingredients except turkey pastrami in a covered pan. Cover and simmer slowly over low heat until peppers are tender, about 20 minutes. Uncover and add turkey pastrami; continue to simmer until most of the liquid evaporates.

Makes four servings, about 180 calories each.

Blue Jean Green Beans with Leaner Wieners™

¾ pound fresh green beans (or 10-ounce package whole green beans, frozen)
6 sliced turkey franks
¾ cup fat-skimmed turkey or chicken broth (homemade or canned)
1 tablespoon peeled, finely minced onion (or 1 teaspoon instant onion)

Wash and tip green beans; leave whole. (Defrost partially, at room temperature, if frozen.) Spray a small nonstick skillet with cooking spray for no-fat frying. Spread sliced turkey franks in a shallow layer and brown over moderate heat. Remove from skillet and set aside. Add remaining ingredients to skillet. Simmer over very low heat, uncovered, until nearly all the liquid evaporates. Stir in turkey franks and heat through.

Makes three servings, about 235 calories each.

FOUR ▶ TURKEY ON THE RANGE

WHAT GIVES top-of-the-range recipes their weighty wallop of calories isn't necessarily such ingredients as potatoes, rice, or pasta . . . or thickeners like flour or cornstarch. The real villain is fat: the fat that's used in browning the meat and the fat in the meat itself. The cuts of meats usually used in slow-simmered dishes are well-larded with fat. And, in contrast to meat that's roasted or broiled, that fat doesn't just melt and drain away. It stays in the pot, in the sauce, and ultimately winds up on your plate . . . and your hips.

Because turkey has only a fraction of the fat found in most meats, the main source of fat and excess calories is eliminated when you make rangetop dishes with turkey instead of other meats. Calorie-saving browning techniques and nonstick cookware can minimize the need for added fat.

The recipes in this section will provide you with inspiration to start you thinking. You can re-create a whole collection of family favorites simply by substituting turkey thigh meat for cubes of beef in any favorite stew or ragout.

Mexican Fruited Turkey Breast

1 turkey breast portion (about 2½ pounds)
  Salt to taste
  optional: red cayenne pepper or chili powder to taste
¼ cup blanched almonds
⅓ cup seedless raisins
½ cup undrained, juice-packed pineapple chunks
⅛ teaspoon cinnamon
⅛ teaspoon ground cloves
1 cup orange juice
2 tablespoons flour

Season turkey breast with salt (and pepper or chili) to taste. Place skin-side up in a nonstick Dutch oven. Bake, uncovered, in preheated 450-degree oven about 20 minutes, until skin is crisp. Drain and discard any fat.

Add nuts, fruits, spices, and ½ cup orange juice. Cover and simmer (or bake in a 325-degree oven) about 1¾ to 2 hours, until meat is tender.

Remove turkey to a serving platter. Combine flour with remaining ½ cup orange juice and stir into sauce. Cook, stirring, until sauce is thick. Pour over turkey. (Garnish with fresh orange sections, if desired.)

Makes eight servings, under 300 calories each.

Mediterranean Turkey Breast with Olives

1 large turkey breast half (about 3 pounds)
2 peeled, chopped onions
1 seeded, sliced green bell pepper
1 16-ounce can chopped stewed tomatoes
¾ teaspoon chili powder (or to taste)
12 thinly sliced pitted black olives
¼ cup juice (from olives)
2 teaspoons salt or garlic salt

Place turkey breast skin-side up in a nonstick Dutch oven. Bake, uncovered, in preheated 450-degree oven 20 to 30 minutes, basting occasionally, until skin is crisp. Drain and discard any fat.

Add remaining ingredients. Lower heat to 350 degrees. Cover and simmer 1 to 1½ hours, until turkey is very tender. Uncover and continue cooking until sauce is reduced. Slice turkey very thinly and top with sauce.

Makes nine servings, about 260 calories each.

Tex-Mex Turkey Rolls

4 turkey tenderloin steaks (about 1 pound)

8 thin slices (4 ounces) extra-sharp Cheddar or American cheese

1 small peeled, minced onion

1 seeded, minced green bell pepper

1 peeled, diced ripe tomato

1 8-ounce can tomato sauce

2 teaspoons lemon juice

1 cup fat-skimmed turkey broth or water

2 teaspoons chili powder (or more, to taste)

¼ teaspoon ground cumin

1 teaspoon dried oregano

Pound turkey tenderloins thin with a meat mallet. Arrange cheese on top of turkey and roll up with cheese inside. Secure with toothpicks, if necessary. Combine remaining ingredients and pour over turkey in a nonstick pot. Heat to boiling; then lower to a simmer. Cover and simmer 15 minutes. Uncover and continue to simmer until sauce is thick.

Makes four servings, about 290 calories each (280 calories each if made with water).

Turkey with "Cream" Sauce

1 large boned turkey thigh, cut into 1½-inch cubes

2 peeled, halved, sliced onions

2 sliced ribs celery

2 pared, sliced carrots

4 ounces sliced fresh or canned undrained mushrooms

½ cup dry sherry

1 cup water

¼ teaspoon poultry seasoning

Salt or garlic salt and pepper to taste

½ teaspoon paprika

1 cup evaporated skim milk

2 tablespoons instant-blending flour

Spray a heavy Dutch oven with cooking spray for no-fat frying. Add turkey, skin-side down. Cook over moderate heat until turkey begins to brown in its own melted fat. Drain and discard any fat.

Add remaining ingredients except evaporated milk and flour. Cover and simmer until turkey is tender, about 1 hour. Uncover and continue to simmer until most of the liquid evaporates. Skim fat.

Combine evaporated milk and flour, then stir into simmering liquid over low heat, cooking until sauce is thick and bubbling. (Garnish with parsley, if desired.)

Makes five servings, about 355 calories each.

Indian Turkey Ragout

2 boned young turkey thighs, cut
    into 1½-inch cubes
    Garlic salt and pepper to taste
1¼ cups fat-skimmed turkey or
    chicken broth
2 tablespoons lemon juice
2 tablespoons soy sauce
4 tablespoons raisins
1 tablespoon curry powder
2 peeled, sliced onions
3 tablespoons flour
2 unpeeled, cored, diced red apples
4 tablespoons defatted or dry-roasted
    peanuts

Spray a nonstick skillet or pressure cooker with cooking spray for no-fat frying. Add turkey cubes, skin-side down, and brown quickly over high heat. Pour off any fat. Season with garlic salt and pepper. Add 1 cup broth, lemon juice, soy sauce, raisins, and curry. Cover and simmer in skillet until tender, 1 hour or more (or pressure cook, according to manufacturer's directions, for 20 minutes).

Skim fat, if any, from surface of broth.

Add onions and simmer, uncovered, 5 minutes. Combine flour with remaining broth and stir into simmering liquid until thick. Stir in apples and peanuts just before serving.

Makes ten servings, about 335 calories each.

Savory Turkey-Potato Ragout

1 boned turkey thigh, cut into 1-inch
    cubes
1 cup tomato juice
1 large peeled, halved, thinly sliced
    onion
    optional: 1 minced clove garlic
1 teaspoon paprika
1 teaspoon dried savory
    Salt and pepper to taste
2 thinly sliced ribs celery
2 scraped, sliced carrots
2 peeled, sliced potatoes
1 teaspoon cornstarch
¼ cup cold water

Coat a large nonstick skillet or electric frypan lightly with oil, or spray with cooking spray for no-fat frying. Add the turkey cubes and brown slowly over moderate heat, turning to prevent sticking. Drain and discard any fat. Add tomato juice, onion, garlic, paprika, savory, salt, and pepper. Lower heat and cover. Simmer until turkey is tender, about 45 minutes to 1 hour. (Add water, if needed.)

Stir in vegetables. Cover and simmer until potatoes are tender, about 20 minutes. Combine cornstarch with water and stir into simmering skillet until thickened.

Makes five servings, about 340 calories each.

Italian Turkey Roll

1 boned turkey thigh
1 minced clove garlic
2 teaspoons dried oregano
1 teaspoon dried basil
  Salt and pepper to taste
2 tablespoons grated Parmesan
    cheese
2 ounces thinly sliced or shredded
    part-skim mozzarella cheese
¼ cup chopped fresh parsley
1 16-ounce can chopped tomatoes
    packed in purée or chopped
    stewed tomatoes
1 cup water
½ cup Chianti or other dry red wine
1 large peeled, chopped onion
½ seeded, diced green bell pepper

Lay boned turkey thigh flat on a cutting board, skin-side out. Sprinkle the inside with garlic, 1 teaspoon oregano, ½ teaspoon basil, salt, pepper, and Parmesan cheese. Add the mozzarella in a single layer. Top with parsley. Roll up skin-side out; tie with white kitchen string.

Spray a nonstick Dutch oven or heavy pot with cooking spray for no-stick frying. Brown the roll, with no fat added, over low heat. Drain and discard any fat. Combine remaining ingredients, adding remaining oregano and basil. Cover and simmer over very low heat until very tender, about 1½ hours. (Add water, if needed.) If sauce is too thin, uncover and simmer down until thick and chunky.

To serve, remove string and slice turkey into thin slices. Top with sauce. (Serve over pasta, if desired.)

Makes five servings, about 365 calories each. (Tender-cooked pasta is about 155 calories per cupful.)

Mexican Flank Roll With Cheddar

Follow recipe for Italian Turkey Roll (above) but replace basil with 2 teaspoons chili powder. Replace Parmesan and mozzarella with 3 ounces extra-sharp Cheddar (or Cheddar-type "diet") cheese. Replace wine with water and add 1 teaspoon vinegar. Use 1 large green bell pepper.

Makes five servings, about 390 calories each; about 350 calories each with diet cheese.

Greek Flank Roll with Feta Cheese

Follow recipe for Italian Turkey Roll (above). Substitute dried mint leaves for oregano. Omit basil. Add ¼ teaspoon ground nutmeg and a dash of cinnamon. Replace cheeses with 3 ounces feta cheese. Replace wine with water and add 2 tablespoons lemon juice.

Makes five servings, about 365 calories each.

Mexican Turkey Roll

1 boned turkey thigh
2 finely minced cloves garlic (or ¼
    teaspoon instant garlic)
1 teaspoon cumin seeds (or ¼
    teaspoon ground cumin)
1 teaspoon oregano or basil
    Salt and pepper to taste
    2 ounces shredded extra-sharp
      Cheddar cheese
1 8-ounce can tomato sauce
2 cups fat-skimmed turkey broth or
    water
1 teaspoon vinegar
1 minced rib celery
1 seeded, diced green bell pepper
1 peeled, chopped onion
2 tablespoons raisins

Spread boned turkey thigh flat, skin-side down. Sprinkle the inside with garlic, cumin, oregano, salt, and pepper. Put the shredded cheese in the center. Roll up, skin-side out; tie with white kitchen twine or secure with toothpicks.

Spray a nonstick skillet, Dutch oven, or pressure cooker with cooking spray for no-fat frying. Brown the turkey roll with no fat added; turn to brown evenly. Discard any fat. Stir in remaining ingredients. Cover and simmer 1½ hours (30 minutes in pressure cooker, according to manufacturer's directions) or until meat is very tender. Uncover and permit sauce to reduce. Spoon sauce over turkey roll. (Serve with rice, if desired.)

Makes five servings, about 365 calories each. (Fluffy rice is about 100 calories per ½-cup serving.)

Spanish Turkey Stew, Gazpacho Style

1 large boned turkey thigh, cut into
    1½-inch cubes
3 tablespoons low-calorie Italian
    salad dressing
1 peeled, chopped onion
1 seeded, sliced green bell pepper
1 16-ounce can stewed tomatoes
1 minced clove garlic
1 bay leaf
    Salt and pepper to taste
½ cup water or beef broth
1 medium sliced zucchini (or 1 10-
    ounce package, frozen)

Combine turkey cubes with salad dressing. Marinate, covered, in the refrigerator for several hours.

Spray a nonstick skillet with cooking spray for no-fat frying. Drain the turkey. Sear turkey in the skillet over high heat, turning to brown evenly. Add remaining ingredients except zucchini. Cover and simmer over very low heat until meat is tender, about 1 hour. Uncover and stir in zucchini. Simmer, uncovered, until most of the liquid evaporates.

Makes five servings, about 315 calories each.

Crocked Turkey, Italian Style

1 skinned, boned turkey thigh, cut
    into 1½-inch cubes
1 large peeled, halved, sliced onion
1 peeled ripe tomato, cut into chunks
1 minced clove garlic
1 green seeded, thinly sliced green
    bell pepper
2 tablespoons lemon juice
1 teaspoon dried basil or mixed
    Italian seasoning
  Salt and pepper to taste

Combine all ingredients in crockpot or slow-cooker. Cook on high setting 30 minutes. Cook 8 to 10 hours or longer on low heat, until meat is very tender.

Makes five servings, about 290 calories each.

Turkey Carbonnade

2 boned turkey thighs cut into 1½-
    inch cubes
1 tablespoon salad oil
  Salt and pepper to taste
½ teaspoon poultry seasoning
2 teaspoons brown sugar
1 cup light (calorie-reduced) beer
4 peeled, thinly sliced onions
½ teaspoon cornstarch
2 tablespoons cold water

Combine turkey cubes and oil. In a nonstick heavy Dutch oven or skillet, brown slowly. Drain and discard any fat. Add seasonings, sugar, and beer. Cover and simmer 1 hour or more, until meat is tender. (Add water, if needed.) Add onions. Cover and simmer 20 minutes. Blend cornstarch and water together and stir into skillet until thickened.

Makes eight servings, about 390 calories each.

Applesauced Turkey

1 boned turkey thigh, cut into 1½-
    inch cubes
2 peeled, sliced onions
  optional: 1 to 2 cloves minced
    garlic
1 cup unsweetened applesauce
1 cup water
  optional: 1½ teaspoons curry
    powder (or to taste)
  Salt and pepper to taste

Spray a nonstick skillet or electric frypan with cooking spray for no-fat frying. Add the turkey cubes skin-side down. Brown on all sides (no fat added). Drain and discard any fat.

Add remaining ingredients. Cover and simmer over low heat until turkey is tender. Uncover. Continue to simmer until sauce is reduced to a thick glaze.

Makes five servings, about 305 calories each.

Turkey in Plum Sauce

1 boned turkey thigh, cut into 1½-inch cubes
6 ripe, fresh, unpeeled, purple plums, pitted and sliced
1 peeled, halved, thinly sliced onion
1 minced clove garlic
2 tablespoons lemon juice
2 tablespoons soy sauce
   optional: 1 tablespoon honey
1 cup water

Arrange turkey cubes skin-side down in a nonstick skillet with no fat added. Cook, uncovered, over medium heat, turning to brown evenly. Drain and discard any fat. Blot turkey and place skin-side up in skillet. Add remaining ingredients. Cover and simmer, stirring occasionally, until turkey is tender, 1 hour or more. (Add water, if needed.) Uncover and simmer until sauce is thick.

Makes five servings, about 325 calories each with honey; about 310 calories each without honey.

Turkey Stifado

1 turkey thigh (about 1½ pound)
4 small peeled, whole onions
1 8-ounce can chopped tomatoes
¾ cup (1 6-ounce can) tomato juice
2 tablespoons cider vinegar
1 minced clove garlic
1 bay leaf
   optional: ¼ teaspoon coriander seeds
Salt and pepper to taste

Brown turkey thigh, skin-side down, in a nonstick Dutch oven with no fat added. Turn to brown evenly. Drain and discard any fat.

Add remaining ingredients. Cover and simmer 2 hours or more, until meat is tender and liquid is reduced to a delicious sauce. Remove bay leaf.

Makes five servings, about 315 calories each.

Turkey Stew Cubano

2 boned turkey thighs, cut into 1-inch cubes
1 16-ounce can undrained, crushed tomatoes
2 peeled, chopped onions
1 minced clove garlic
3 sliced ribs celery
3 tablespoons raisins
1 tablespoon vinegar
⅓ cup water or fat-skimmed turkey broth
   Salt and pepper to taste
   Pinch of ground cloves
¼ teaspoon chili powder (or more, to taste)
12 stuffed green (Spanish) olives, sliced

Spray a large electric skillet, frypan, or heavy Dutch oven with cooking spray for no-fat frying. Add the turkey cubes, skin-side down. Brown over high heat with no fat added. Turn frequently to prevent sticking. Drain fat, if any, from pan.

Add remaining ingredients except olives. Cover and simmer over low heat 2 hours or until meat is tender. Uncover and allow to simmer down, until nearly all the liquid is evaporated. Stir in olives and heat through.

(Serve with cooked brown rice, if desired.)

Makes ten servings, about 305 calories each with water; about 310 calories each with broth. (A ½ cup cooked brown rice adds about 90 calories.)

Turkey Stroganoff Roll with Noodles

1 boned turkey thigh
1 tablespoon prepared mustard
2 teaspoons Worcestershire sauce
  optional: 1 small minced clove
    garlic (or pinch of instant
    garlic)
  Pepper to taste
¼ cup minced fresh parsley
3 cups tomato juice
1 largel peeled, chopped onion
½ cup dry white wine or water
1 cup water
4 ounces (dry) ruffle-edge noodles
½ cup plain low-fat yogurt

Spread boned turkey thigh flat, skin-side down. Spread the inside lightly with mustard and sprinkle with Worcestershire sauce, garlic, pepper, and half the parsley. Roll up with the seasonings inside. Secure with toothpicks or tie with kitchen twine. Brown the roll in a nonstick skillet sprayed with cooking spray for no-stick frying. Turn to brown evenly. Discard any fat. Add tomato juice, onion, wine, and water. Cover and simmer 1½ hours.

Uncover and stir in noodles, a few at a time, so mixture continues to simmer. Cover and simmer 10 to 15 minutes or more, stirring frequently, until noodles are tender and sauce is thick. Stir in yogurt and remaining minced parsley, just until heated through.

Makes five servings, about 420 calories each.

Texas Turkey Chili

2 skinned, boned turkey thighs
    (about 3 pounds), cut into 1-
    inch cubes
2 teaspoons salad oil
1 cup fat-skimmed turkey or chicken
    broth
1 28-ounce can tomatoes, including
    liquid
2 large peeled, chopped onions
4 seeded, chopped green bell
    peppers
2 minced cloves garlic
1 tablespoon chili powder (or to
    taste)
2 teaspoons cumin seeds
2 teaspoons dried oregano
  Salt and pepper to taste
  optional: ¼ cup shredded extra-
    sharp Cheddar, Jack, or
    American cheese

Spray a nonstick saucepan with cooking spray for no-fat cooking. Add turkey and oil. Brown over moderate heat. Drain and discard any fat.

Add all remaining ingredients except cheese. Cover and simmer over low heat until turkey is very tender, about 1 hour (or 20 minutes in pressure cooker, according to manufacturer's instructions). Uncover; continue to simmer until most of the liquid evaporates and chili is thick. Spoon into serving dish. Top with shredded cheese, if desired.

Makes ten servings, about 315 calories each with cheese; about 325 calories each without cheese.

Roast Turkey "Waikiki"

1 turkey hindquarter (about 3½ pounds)
½ teaspoon poultry seasoning
1 8-ounce can undrained, juice-packed crushed pineapple
1 cup fat-skimmed turkey or chicken broth
½ teaspoon cinnamon
Salt and pepper to taste

Place turkey skin-side up in a nonstick baking pan. Sprinkle with poultry seasoning. Bake in preheated 450-degree oven 20 to 25 minutes, until skin is crisp. Drain and discard any fat.

Combine remaining ingredients. Pour over turkey. Lower heat to 325 degrees. Cover and bake about 1 hour, until tender. Uncover and continue to bake until sauce is thick.

Makes ten servings, about 350 calories each.

Turkey Meat Sauce for Pasta

2 turkey drumsticks
4 cups water
1 12-ounce can tomato paste
2 medium peeled, chopped onions
1 4-ounce can drained mushrooms
2 teaspoons oregano
1 tablespoon minced fresh parsley
1 minced clove garlic (or ¼ teaspoon instant garlic)
Salt and pepper to taste
3 tablespoons grated Parmesan cheese

Place drumsticks in large pot; cover with water. Bring to boil; reduce heat; cover and simmer 1½ hours. Remove turkey from broth and cool slightly. Remove meat from bones and set aside.

Skim any fat from broth. Combine broth with tomato paste and stir until blended. Add onions, mushrooms, oregano, parsley, garlic, and seasonings. Cover and simmer 10 minutes. Add reserved turkey meat and heat through. Serve over pasta (or noodles or rice), if desired, and sprinkle with cheese.

Makes eight servings, about 245 calories each. (Tender-cooked spaghetti is about 155 calories per cupful; tender-cooked noodles are about 200 calories per cupful; each ½ cup fluffy rice adds about 100 calories.)

Turkey Osso Buco

2 young turkey drumsticks
2 cups water
½ cup dry white wine
1 16-ounce can chopped tomatoes
2 peeled, sliced onions
1 large scraped, sliced carrot
2 sliced ribs celery
1 minced clove garlic (or ⅛ teaspoon
   instant garlic)
1 bay leaf
1 teaspoon basil or mixed Italian
   seasoning
  Salt and pepper to taste
2 tablespoons chopped fresh parsley
1 teaspoon grated lemon rind

Combine turkey, water, and ¼ cup wine in a heavy Dutch oven (or pressure cooker). Cover and cook until turkey is tender, about 1½ hours (or 30 minutes under pressure, according to manufacturer's directions). Remove turkey from broth and allow to cool. Separate meat from bones and dice into bite-size pieces. Discard skin and bones.

Skim fat from broth. Combine broth with ¼ cup wine and remaining ingredients except parsley and lemon rind. Cover and simmer over very low heat until carrots are tender, about 20 minutes (7 minutes under pressure).

Return meat to pot. Uncover and continue to simmer until sauce is very thick. Sprinkle with parsley and lemon rind.

Makes six servings, about 285 calories each.

Turkey with Pineapple Kraut

2 turkey drumsticks
2 cups water
1 peeled, sliced onion
1 8-ounce can undrained, juice-
   packed pineapple chunks
4 cups rinsed, drained sauerkraut
  Salt and pepper to taste

Place drumsticks in kettle, cover with water, and simmer 1 hour. Skim fat with bulb-type baster. Add onion, pineapple juice (reserving pineapple chunks), and sauerkraut. Cover and simmer until turkey is so tender that the meat separates easily from the bones. (Add water, if needed.) Remove bones and skin before serving. Season to taste. Add pineapple chunks and heat through.

Makes eight meal-size servings, about 220 calories each.

Turkey Tarragon

4 tablespoons flour
  Seasoned salt and pepper to taste
4 turkey drumettes (first portion of
   wing)
1 teaspoon dried tarragon

Combine flour, seasoned salt, and pepper in a heavy brown paper bag. Add drumettes. Close bag tightly and shake up, until drumettes are lightly coated. Arrange drumettes in a single layer in a nonstick baking pan. Bake, uncovered, in preheated 475-

½ cup dry white wine
3 small bunches chopped green
　　onions (scallions)
½ pound sliced fresh mushrooms

degree oven 20 to 30 minutes, until skin is crisp and brown. Drain and discard any fat.

Sprinkle drumettes with tarragon; add wine. Cover tightly. Lower heat to 350 degrees and bake until tender, about 50 to 60 minutes. Uncover and add scallions and mushrooms. Continue to bake, uncovered, stirring mushrooms occasionally, until most of the liquid evaporates.

Makes six servings, about 335 calories each.

Turkey Spaghetti and Meatballs

1 pound ground turkey
¼ cup minced fresh parsley
½ teaspoon dried basil
　　Salt and pepper to taste
1 cup fat-skimmed turkey broth
1 18-ounce can Italian tomatoes
1 6-ounce can tomato paste
1 cup peeled, chopped onion
½ cup chopped green bell pepper
½ cup chopped celery
1 minced clove garlic
1½ teaspoons dried oregano
½ pound (dry) spaghetti

Combine turkey with parsley, basil, salt, and pepper. Shape into sixteen meatballs and brown under high heat in broiler, turning once.

Combine remaining ingredients except spaghetti together in a saucepan. Heat to boiling. Add meatballs. Cover and simmer over low heat for 40 to 50 minutes. Uncover; simmer until sauce is gravy-thick. Meanwhile, cook spaghetti according to package directions.

Makes six servings, about 490 calories each.

Turkey-Eggplant Chili

1 pound turkey breakfast sausage or
　　ground turkey
1 medium pared, diced eggplant
1 large peeled, minced onion
3 seeded, diced green bell peppers
1 6-ounce can tomato paste
1½ cups fat-skimmed turkey broth
　　to 2 minced cloves garlic (or ¼
　　　　teaspoon instant garlic)
　　Salt and pepper to taste
1 tablespoon chili powder (or more,
　　to taste)
½ cup shredded sharp Cheddar
　　cheese

Brown turkey sausage in large nonstick skillet with no fat added. Break into chunks as it browns. Pour off any fat. Stir in remaining ingredients except cheese. Cover tightly and simmer over very low heat 1 hour or more. Sprinkle with cheese before serving.

Makes four servings, about 370 calories each (360 calories each with ground turkey).

FIVE ▶ TURKEY OVER THE COALS OR UNDER THE BROILER

Every calorie-cautious cook knows that broiling and barbecuing are the best ways to cook. The sight of all that fat dripping into the coals is reassuring evidence that calories are going up into smoke. What broiler fans and backyard chefs neglect to think about is that the meats usually chosen for broiling and barbecuing tend to be the most calorie-laden of all: fatty steaks and chops, greasy burgers and franks. And what you see is only a fraction of what you get. Some of the fat melts away, but most of it doesn't!

If you'd rather wear a bikini than a muu-muu to a cookout, discover the turkey alternative. Today's turkey comes in steaks and franks, ground into burgers and cut into parts and portions just right for the broiler or backyard barbecue. And versatile turkey adapts happily to all your favorite flavoring marinades and bastes.

Speaking of marinades and bastes, why squander calories needlessly on large amounts of oil (or other ingredients) that do little except inflate the calorie count?

Let's consider the purpose of marinades and basting sauces:

▶ to moisten and prevent burning—liquid basting sauces help prevent the evaporation of meat juices when the surface is exposed to the high heat of hot coals or the broiler flame.

▶ to flavor—zesty sauces, spices, and seasonings add a flavor accent or counterpoint to the flavor of the food being broiled or barbecued. Spices and herbs have virtually no calories.

92

▶ to tenderize—marinating meat in an acid liquid (wine; vinegar; tomato juice; lemon, orange, pineapple, or other fruit juice) helps to tenderize and soften the meat fibers.

You'll notice that the addition of oil or fat serves no real purpose in marinades and basting sauces. Oil has no flavor, doesn't tenderize, and adds no moisture. It's the acid liquid, the spices, herbs, and seasonings that consitute the "business end" of a basting sauce.

Tips for Low-Calorie Basting Sauces and Marinades

Follow any favorite recipe but reduce or eliminate all oil. Every tablespoon of oil you delete saves you 115 to 125 calories. Increase the volume of juice, or other liquids called for, to make up the proper amount.

If your favorite basting sauce calls for the use of commercial salad dressing, subsitute the low-calorie, low-fat "diet" versions instead.

Watch out for basting sauces that include large amounts of sugar, honey, molasses, and other refined sweets. A cupful of sugar is 750 calories. The baste may outweigh the turkey in calories if you're too heavy-handed with sweeteners. Try cutting the amount of sugar in half; for a taste of Mother Nature's sweetness, substitute naturally sweet fruit juices or fruit-juice concentrates.

Most other flavoring ingredients are calorie lightweights: soy sauce, mustard, Worcestershire sauce, garlic, onion, chili, and curry, all spices and herbs, fruit juices, vinegar, and wine. Remember, the alcohol calories *do* go up in smoke!

Casino Marinade

½ cup dry white wine
½ cup low-calorie French dressing
2 teaspoons prepared mustard
   optional: 2 teaspoons brown sugar
1 teaspoon garlic salt
1 tablespoon lemon juice

Combine all ingredients and blend well. Use as a marinade for turkey.

Makes 1 cup, about 150 calories (180 calories with brown sugar).

Chinese-Style Barbecue Sauce

1 cup sliced peaches (fresh or
   drained, juice-packed)
2 tablespoons brown sugar
2 tablespoons catsup
2 tablespoons soy sauce
3 cloves garlic
2 teaspoons chopped fresh ginger (or
   1 teaspoon ground ginger)

Combine ingredients in blender and blend on high speed until smooth. Use as a basting sauce for turkey.

Makes 1 cup, about 240 calories with fresh peaches; 275 calories with canned peaches.

Deviled Marinade for Turkey

¾ cup (1 6-ounce can) tomato juice
2 teaspoons prepared mustard
2 teaspoons Worcestershire sauce
3 tablespoons catsup
¼ teaspoon red hot pepper sauce
   Garlic salt and pepper to taste

Combine ingredients. Use as a marinade or baste.
Makes 1 cup, about 110 calories.

Mexican Barbecue Sauce for Turkey

¼ cup water
¼ cup vinegar
1½ tablespoons peeled, minced onion
1½ tablespoons minced green bell
   pepper
½ cup catsup
½ teaspoon oregano
1 teaspoon chili powder
1 minced clove garlic
   Salt and pepper to taste

Combine all ingredients and simmer for 5 minutes.
Makes about 1 cup, about 11 calories per tablespoon.

Polynesian Hot Curry Marinade

⅓ cup soy sauce
½ cup orange juice
1 tablespoon lemon juice
3 tablespoons low-sugar apricot jam
1 tablespoon curry powder
1 teaspoon red cayenne pepper
1 tablespoon dried onion flakes

Combine ingredients and use as a baste for turkey. Makes 1 cup, about 190 calories.

Trim Teriyaki Marinade

½ cup soy sauce
½ cup saki or dry sherry
2 minced cloves garlic (or ¼ teaspoon garlic powder)
1 teaspoon ground ginger or 1 tablespoon chopped fresh ginger
1 teaspoon dried parsley flakes
optional: 1 teaspoon liquid smoke seasoning

Combine ingredients. Use as a marinade. Makes 1 cup, about 100 calories.

Polynesian "Sweet and Sour" Turkey Marinade

½ cup red-wine vinegar
1 6-ounce can defrosted, undiluted pineapple juice concentrate
3 tablespoons catsup
1 tablespoon soy sauce
1 teaspoon dry mustard
1 cup undrained, juice-packed crushed pineapple
½ seeded, minced green bell pepper
2 teaspoons cornstarch
¼ cup cold water

Combine all ingredients except cornstarch and water in a saucepan. Bring to boil, then simmer for 5 minutes. Blend cornstarch and water until smooth. Add to mixture, stirring until sauce thickens. Use as a marinade or basting sauce for turkey.
Makes 3 cups, about 15 calories per tablespoon.

Fat-free Barbecue Sauce for Turkey

1 8-ounce can tomato sauce
1 tablespoon lemon juice
2 teaspoons honey (or 1 tablespoon brown sugar)
1 tablespoon Worcestershire sauce
1 minced clove garlic (or pinch of instant garlic)
½ teaspoon dried oregano or basil

Stir all ingredients together.

In a covered bowl, marinate cubes of raw turkey in the mixture all day or overnight in the refrigerator. Or use as a barbecue baste for turkeyburgers.

Sauce makes six servings, about 20 calories each.

Barbecue Sauce for Cut-up Turkey Parts

1 clove crushed garlic
¾ teaspoon salt
½ teaspoon pepper
¼ cup minced onion
1 teaspoon prepared mustard
½ teaspoon dry mustard
1 tablespoon lemon juice
1 cup tomato sauce
Dash of Tabasco
optional: 1 tablespoon sugar or 2 teaspoons honey

Combine all the ingredients in blender or food processor. Cover and blend till smooth. Makes about 1¼ cups sauce. Baste the turkey parts during last half hour of grilling or roasting.

Makes six servings, about 15 calories each (sugar or honey adds 10 calories per serving).

Polynesian BBQ Breast Portion

1 turkey breast portion (about 2 pounds)
3 cups Polynesian "Sweet and Sour" Turkey Marinade (p. 95)

Marinate turkey in marinade for several hours, covered, in the refrigerator. Turn occasionally. Barbecue 6 inches from coals, turning often; or secure on rotisserie. Baste frequently with reserved marinade. Cook 1 hour or more, until tender.

Makes six servings, about 340 calories each.

Marinated Turkey Steaks

Turkey tenderloin steaks (about 4 ounces each)
Your choice of marinade

Spread turkey steaks with your choice of marinade. Puncture both sides with a fork (or angelfood-cake cutter). Cover and marinate all day or overnight in refrigerator.

POLYNESIAN: use equal parts soy sauce and defrosted pineapple juice concentrate. Add a pinch of ground ginger. (Frozen pineapple juice has an enzyme that breaks down meat fibers.) About 85 calories per ¼ cup.

LEMON ITALIAN: use 1 tablespoon lemon juice per steak. Sprinkle with dried basil or oregano and chopped fresh garlic to taste. About 5 calories per tablespoon.

WINE ITALIAN: use commercial low-fat Italian salad dressing thinned with an equal amount of dry red wine. About 6 calories per tablespoon.

TOMATO ITALIAN: cover the steaks with tomato juice, sprinkle with dried basil or oregano and chopped garlic (optional). Drain well before cooking steaks. Put the reserved juice in a skillet and simmer down over high heat to make a sauce. Tomato juice is about 12 calories per ¼ cup.

BARBECUE: cover steaks with Bloody Mary-seasoned tomato juice (15 calories per ¼ cup.) Drain steaks and pan-fry with 1 teaspoon salad oil (41 calories per teaspoon). Remove steaks. Put juice in skillet and cook over high heat until reduced. Pour over steaks.

Turkey on Skewers with Polynesian Marinade

1 pound turkey breast tenderloin or tenderloin steaks

POLYNESIAN BLENDER MARINADE:

½ cup dry white wine
⅓ cup water
4 tablespoons soy sauce
   optional: 1 tablespoon honey
1 teaspoon curry powder
1 cup peeled, sliced onion
2 cloves garlic

Slice turkey into 2-inch cubes. Put the meat in a plastic bag and put bag in a bowl to catch any leaks.

Combine marinade ingredients in blender (or food processor, using the steel blade). Cover and blend to a purée. Pour purée over turkey and mix well. Refrigerate all day or overnight.

Thread turkey on skewers. Broil or barbecue 3 inches from heat source, turning frequently, until cooked through. Baste with reserved marinade as meat cooks.

Makes four servings, about 160 calories each; about 175 calories each with honey.

Turkey à la Grecque en Brochette

1 pound turkey tenderloin, cut into
   1½-inch cubes
¼ cup lemon juice
1 minced clove garlic (or ⅛ teaspoon
   instant garlic)
1 teaspoon dried oregano or mint
¼ teaspoon apple pie spice
2 teaspoons olive oil

Combine all ingredients except oil in a glass or plastic bowl. Cover and marinate 24 hours in the refrigerator.

Thread turkey cubes on skewers, reserving marinade. Add oil to remaining marinade, and brush turkey.

Broil or barbecue 3 inches from heat source about 10 to 15 minutes, turning occasionally. Brush turkey with marinade each time it is turned.

Makes four servings, about 160 calories each.

Turkish Turkey en Brochette

4 turkey tenderloin steaks (about 1
   pound)
4 tablespoons lemon juice
2 tablespoons steak sauce, catsup, or
   chili sauce
2 or 3 small bay leaves
1 large seeded green bell pepper, cut
   into 1-inch squares
4 small peeled, halved onions
¼ pound small fresh mushrooms
1 tablespoon salad oil

Cut steaks into 1½-inch cubes. Combine turkey in a glass bowl or plastic bag with lemon juice, steak sauce, and bay leaves. (Add a little cold water, if needed, so that turkey pieces are uniformly moistened.) Refrigerate all day or overnight.

Thread turkey on skewers, alternating with pepper, onion, and mushrooms. Brush very lightly with oil. Broil or barbecue 3 inches from heat source, turning frequently, about 10 to 15 minutes. Brush with reserved marinade while turning.

Makes four servings, about 215 calories each.

Turkey and Pineapple on Skewers

1 turkey breast tenderloin or
   tenderloin steak
1 16-ounce can undrained, juice-
   packed pineapple chunks
2 tablespoons regular or low-calorie
   Italian salad dressing
1 tablespoon soy or Worcestershire
   sauce
¼ teaspoon cinnamon or apple pie
   spice
   Salt and pepper to taste

Cut turkey into 1½-inch chunks. Thread on skewers, alternating with pineapple. (Reserve the juice.) Brush with salad dressing. Broil or barbecue 3 inches from heat source, turning frequently, about 15 to 20 minutes.

Meanwhile, combine reserved pineapple juice with soy or Worcestershire sauce and spice in a small saucepan. Simmer down, uncovered, to a thick glaze. Spoon over turkey and pineapple just before serving.

Makes six servings, about 205 calories each with regular salad dressing; 180 calories each with low-calorie dressing.

Marinated Spiced Turkey Tenderloin

2 tablespoons mixed pickling spices
1 minced clove garlic (or ⅛ teaspoon
  instant garlic)
4 turkey breast tenderloin steaks
  (about 1 pound)
½ cup vinegar
2 teaspoons salad oil

Sprinkle half the pickling spices and garlic in a shallow pan. Add turkey steaks in a single layer. Sprinkle turkey steaks with remaining spices and garlic. Add vinegar and just enough water to cover. Cover the dish and refrigerate all day or overnight.

Drain turkey. Brush lightly with oil. Barbacue or broil 3 inches from heat source, turning once, until cooked through.

Makes four servings, about 160 calories each.

Chinese Broiled Turkey Breast Steaks

4 turkey breast tenderloin steaks
  (about 1 pound)
1 teaspoon grated fresh ginger (or
  pinch of ground ginger)
1 teaspoon dry mustard
  optional: 1 teaspoon MSG
  optional: 1 tablespoon honey
½ cup soy sauce
¼ cup sherry or water
2 minced cloves garlic
2 teaspoons salad oil

Put turkey steaks in a plastic bag. Add all ingredients except oil. Refrigerate several hours. Remove steaks from marinade and brush lightly with oil. Barbecue or broil 3 inches from heat source 4 to 5 minutes each side, brushing occasionally with reserved marinade.

Makes four servings, about 195 calories each (honey adds 15 calories per serving).

Italian Turkeybob

1 pound turkey breast tenderloin or
  tenderloin steaks
1 cup regular or low-calorie Italian
  salad dressing
4 small peeled, quartered onions
2 small thickly sliced fresh zucchini
  (about 1 inch slices)
1 red bell pepper, cut into 1-inch
  squares

Cut turkey into 1-inch cubes. Marinate in salad dressing all day or overnight, covered, in the refrigerator. Alternate turkey, onions, zucchini, and red pepper on skewers. Broil or barbecue 3 inches from heat source, brushing with reserved marinade, until turkey is cooked through, 10 to 15 minutes. Turn frequently.

Makes four servings, about 510 calories each; about 210 calories each with low-calorie dressing.

Ginger Barbecue Sauce for Turkey

½ cup soy sauce
½ cup dry sherry or other white wine
½ cup catsup
1 tablespoon fresh grated ginger (or 1 teaspoon ground ginger)
1 crushed clove garlic (or ⅛ teaspoon instant garlic)

Combine ingredients and use as a flavoring marinade or barbecue basting sauce for turkey.

Makes 1½ cups, about 11 calories per tablespoon.

Ginger BBQ Turkey

2 skinned, boned turkey thighs, cut into 2-inch cubes
1½ cups Ginger BBQ Sauce for Turkey (above)

Marinate turkey meat in Ginger BBQ sauce 2 hours or more in the refrigerator. Thread cubes on skewers. Broil or barbecue 5 inches from heat source, basting often with reserved sauce. Turn frequently. Cook 45 minutes or more, until tender.

Makes ten servings, under 300 calories each.

Sour Creamy Marinade for Turkey Drumettes

1 cup sour cream or plain low-fat yogurt
2 mashed cloves garlic
1 teaspoon Worcestershire sauce
1 tablespoon lemon juice
½ teaspoon salt
1 teaspoon paprika
¼ teaspoon pepper
4 turkey drumettes (first portion of wing)

Combine all ingredients except turkey, and mix well. Pour marinade over turkey drumettes. Cover and refrigerate overnight. Shake off excess marinade before cooking.

Broil or barbecue 5 to 6 inches from heat source, turning frequently, 50 to 60 minutes. Baste occasionally with reserved marinade during the last 10 minutes.

Makes six servings, about 375 calories with sour cream; about 315 calories with yogurt.

Barbecued Turkey Necks

5 turkey necks
1 cup water
⅓ cup cider vinegar
1 tablespoon Worcestershire sauce

Combine turkey necks with water and vinegar in a deep pot. Cover and simmer 45 minutes. Skim fat from broth. Combine broth with remaining ingredients and mix well to make basting sauce.

½ teaspoon onion salt
¼ teaspoon garlic salt
½ teaspoon pepper
  optional: 2 teaspoons honey
½ cup catsup

Coat partially cooked necks with basting sauce. Barbecue or broil 6 inches from heat source 20 to 30 minutes. Turn and baste frequently.

Makes about five servings, about 395 calories each. (Honey adds about 10 calories per serving.)

Greek Turkeyburgers

1 pound ground turkey
1 tablespoon lemon juice
  Onion or garlic salt and pepper to taste
¼ teaspoon cinnamon
⅛ teaspoon nutmeg
1 teaspoon dried mint
1 cup tomato juice

Combine turkey, lemon juice, seasonings, and just enough tomato juice to moisten. Shape into four patties. Broil or barbecue 3 inches from heat source, turning once and basting with remaining tomato juice.

Makes four servings, about 220 calories each.

Lemon Turkeyburgers

1 slice dry bread (diet or high-fiber bread may be used)
1 pound ground turkey
1 lightly beaten egg (or 2 egg whites or ¼ cup defrosted no-cholesterol substitute)
1 tablespoon chili sauce or catsup
½ teaspoon cumin seeds
1 minced clove garlic (or ⅛ teaspoon instant garlic)
2 tablespoons chopped fresh mint or parsley
2 tablespoons lemon juice

In blender or with a rolling pin, crush the bread into crumbs. Combine crumbs with remaining ingredients except lemon juice. Toss lightly; then gently shape into four patties. Broil or barbecue 3 inches from heat source, turning once, until cooked through. Baste with lemon juice. (Garnish with additional mint or parsley, if desired.)

Makes four servings, about 250 calories each (240 calories each with egg whites or substitute).

Savory Turkeyburgers

1 pound ground turkey
Salt and pepper to taste
optional: few drops liquid smoke
    seasoning or smoke-flavored
    salt, pinch of cayenne pepper
1 teaspoon dried sage
½ teaspoon dried savory
¼ teaspoon grated nutmeg

Combine ingredients and mix lightly. Gently shape into eight patties. Broil or barbecue 3 inches from heat source 2 minutes on each side.

Each patty, about 105 calories.

Turkey Roquefortburgers

1 pound ground turkey
½ small peeled, finely minced onion
½ cup regular or low-calorie
    Roquefort or blue cheese salad
    dressing

Combine and shape into four burgers. Broil or barbeque 3 inches from heat source, turning once.

Makes four servings, about 390 calories each; about 240 calories each with low-calorie dressing.

Spicy Curried Turkey Sausage

1 pound turkey breakfast sausage
½ cup plain low-fat yogurt (or ½ cup
    evaporated skim milk plus 1
    teaspoon lemon juice)
1 medium peeled, minced onion
½ teaspoon ground cinnamon
⅛ teaspoon ground cloves
    optional: ¼ teaspoon ground
    cardamom or coriander
½ teaspoon chili powder
⅛ teaspoon ground ginger
Salt to taste

Combine ingredients and mix lightly. Shape into four patties. Broil or barbecue 3 inches from heat source, until cooked through. (Baste with tomato juice, if desired.)

Makes four servings, about 250 calories each.

Turkey Cumin Sausage

2 slices dry or toasted bread (high-
    fiber bread may be used)
1 pound turkey breakfast sausage

Soak the bread in water, then squeeze out moisture. Break up moistened bread and combine with remaining ingredients except lemon. Broil or barbe-

1 beaten egg (or 2 egg whites or ¼
    cup defrosted no-cholesterol
    substitute)
1 peeled, finely chopped onion
1 teaspoon cumin seeds (or ½
    teaspoon ground cumin)
  Salt or garlic salt and pepper to
    taste
optional: lemon wedges

cue, turning once, about 6 to 8 minutes. (Serve with lemon wedges, if desired.)

Makes six servings, about 185 calories each.

Turkey Hamsteak Hawaiian

1 pound turkey ham, cut into 4 thick
    slices
1 cup well-drained, juice-packed
    crushed pineapple

Barbecue turkey ham slices 3 inches from heat source until underside is nicely browned. Turn ham over to grill other side. Spread browned side of ham with well-drained pineapple. When underside is browned, transfer ham to a serving platter.

Makes four servings, about 190 calories each.

SIX ▶ TURKEY AWAY FROM IT ALL

WHETHER your "great escape" is a chalet in the mountains or a cottage by the beach, a camper, cabin cruiser, or condominium, today's turkey is a helpful traveling companion when the only one who doesn't get "away from it all" is the cook. Even the best vacation places are likely to be short on space, equipment, utensils, and provisions. Your cupboard (if you have one) is likely to be bare, except for a few canned foods. And though the refrigerator works, it's empty.

If you've got an eat-out kitchen and an eat-in family, today's heat-and-eat turkey products can help you create delicious and nutritious alternatives to warmed-up canned beans.

In this section, we've put together recipes that can help you make short work of galley duty: Dishes that combine easy-to-use turkey products with the types of nonperishable foods likely to be on hand in your summer place.

Here are some suggestions for away-from-home cooks that we've gathered from our own experiences in boating and motor home camping:

▶ A pressure cooker cooks in one-third the time and makes short work of meal preparation, without heating up the galley or kitchen. Use it for one-dish dinners that include vegetables, and cut down on clean-up!

▶ Pack frozen and perishable foods in the same insulated container for the trip from home. The frozen foods keep the perishables chilled.

▶ Keep your second home's kitchen stocked with nonperishables that can

104

be used as ingredients to create a meal: canned tomatoes and potatoes, "instant" rice, canned broths and creamed soups for sauces, nonfat dry milk, canned evaporated skim milk, onion and garlic flakes . . . and wine!

▶ Spices, herbs, and seasonings make the difference between mundane and marvelous, but if storage space is limited, repackage favorite seasonings in small space-saving pill bottles with stick-on labels. Or, combine your own premixed blends for favorite dishes.

▶ Use nonstick cookware to simplify clean-up as well as cut calories and the need for added fat.

▶ Prepare fresh salad ingredients at home. Chop, tear, mince, dice, and toss *without* washing. Pack them in a plastic bag without dressing. Take out just what you need at every meal; wash and crisp the ingredients in cold water before draining and dressing them. (Oil and vinegar need no refrigeration.)

▶ Such products as sliced smoked turkey and turkey ham, pastrami, and bologna are ready-to-eat in sandwiches and salads, or easy-to-heat in a nonstick skillet. Combine them creatively with canned soups and vegetables for hearty meals. Always be sure they are kept refrigerated.

▶ If the weather turns chilly, a quick no-work meal that hits the spot is steamy vegetable soup (from a can) with diced turkey ham or turkey bologna added. Turkey salami heated with canned or packaged macaroni and cheese adds lean protein to an otherwise mostly starch dish.

Ten-minute Turkey Creole

1 16-ounce can chopped stewed
   tomatoes
1 8-ounce can tomato sauce
1 cup water
1 peeled, chopped onion
1 finely chopped rib celery
1 teaspoon chili powder
¼ teaspoon mixed poultry seasoning
1 cup dry "instant" rice
2 cups (about 10 ounces) diced
   cooked turkey

Combine all ingredients except rice and turkey in a saucepan. Cover and simmer 5 minutes. Add rice and turkey. Reheat to boiling. Remove from heat and let stand 5 minutes or more. Fluff before serving.

Makes four servings, about 260 calories each.

Hawaiian Turkey Steaks

4 juice-packed canned pineapple
   rings
¼ cup unsweetened pineapple juice
   (from can)
2 tablespoons soy sauce
1 tablespoon vinegar
4 turkey tenderloin steaks (about 1
   pound)
1 tablespoon salad oil

Combine pineapple juice, soy sauce, and vinegar, pour over turkey. Cover and refrigerate several hours (Or chill, then pack in a leak-proof insulated container.)

Remove the steaks from the marinade and brush lightly with oil. Broil or barbecue 3 inches from heat source about 20 minutes, turning once. Place pineapple rings on broiler rack during the last 5 minutes of cooking; turn once. Serve turkey garnished with pineapple rings.

Makes four servings, about 205 calories each.

Chili con Turkey

½ pound ground turkey
2 peeled, chopped onions
1 seeded, chopped green bell pepper
1 minced clove garlic
1 16-ounce can tomatoes
3 cups canned, drained kidney beans
2 teaspoons chili powder (or more,
   to taste)
  optional: 1 teaspoon cumin seeds
  Salt to taste

Brown turkey lightly in a nonstick skillet with no fat added. Stir in all remaining ingredients. Cover and simmer 25 minutes. Uncover and continue cooking until thickened.

Makes six servings, about 210 calories each.

Mushroom Turkeyburgers

1 pound ground turkey
1 2-ounce can drained, chopped
    mushroom pieces
Pinch of hot pepper
2 tablespoons catsup

Combine all ingredients and shape into four patties. Broil or barbecue 3 inches from heat source, turning once.

Makes four servings, about 220 calories each.

One-pan Turkeyburger Stroganoff

1 pound ground turkey
1 tablespoon margarine or diet
    margarine
    optional: 1 cup peeled, thinly
      sliced onion
2 cups tomato juice
1 4-ounce can drained mushrooms
3 cups fat-skimmed turkey broth
1 teaspoon prepared mustard
    Salt or garlic salt and pepper
4 ounces (dry) ruffle-edged noodles
    (½ package)
½ cup plain low-fat yogurt

Brown turkey in margarine in a nonstick skillet. Add onion, tomato juice, mushrooms, broth, and seasonings. Cook until boiling. Add noodles a few at a time. Cover and simmer until most of the liquid is evaporated. Stir in yogurt; heat over low flame but do not boil.

Makes four servings, about 425 calories each; about 415 calories with diet margarine.

Turkey Salami Skillet Pronto

1 8-ounce can tomato sauce with
    onion (no oil)
½ cup water or dry white wine
¼ teaspoon dried oregano or mixed
    Italian seasoning
1 10-ounce package frozen zucchini
1 10-ounce package frozen kitchen-
    cut green beans
1 pound sliced turkey salami, cut
    into julienne strips

Combine tomato sauce, water or wine, seasonings, and vegetables in a nonstick skillet. Cover and cook 3 minutes. Uncover and break up vegetables with a fork, stirring well. Continue cooking until vegetables are tender. Add turkey salami and heat through.

Makes four servings, about 285 calories each.

One-Pan Italian Turkey Pastrami and Noodles

4 cups fat-skimmed turkey broth (or 4 cups boiling water and 4 cubes or envelopes beef bouillon)
1 6-ounce can tomato paste
   optional: ¼ cup Chianti or other dry red wine
1 2-ounce can mushroom stems and pieces, including liquid
   optional: 1 minced clove garlic
1 peeled, chopped onion
   optional: 1 seeded, chopped green bell pepper
1 teaspoon dried oregano or mixed Italian seasoning
1 pound unsliced turkey pastrami
4 ounces (dry) wide egg noodles

Heat broth to boiling. (If using bouillon, add to water and stir until dissolved.) Stir in tomato paste until smooth. Stir in all remaining ingredients except pastrami and noodles. Heat to boiling. Stir in noodles gradually, to retain simmering. Simmer, stirring frequently, until noodles are very tender and sauce is thick, about 15 minutes. Cut pastrami into 1-inch cubes and stir into pot. Heat through. Spoon into individual plates. (Sprinkle with grated cheese, if desired.)

Makes four servings, about 305 calories each.

Curried Turkey Frankebobs with Pineapple

1 pound turkey franks
1 8-ounce can undrained, juice-packed pineapple chunks
2 bell peppers (1 red, 1 green), cut into 1-inch squares
¼ cup soy sauce
2 teaspoons curry powder
1 teaspoon salad oil

Slice franks into bite-size chunks. Combine all ingredients except oil. Cover and refrigerate all day. (Or chill, then pack in a leak-proof insulated container.) Drain and alternate foods on skewers. Brush lightly with oil. Broil or barbecue 3 inches from heat source 5 to 6 minutes, turning once.

Makes four servings, about 325 calories each.

SEVEN ▶ TURKEY FOR ONE, TWO . . . OR QUITE A FEW

Because of its economy and good value, turkey has always been a traditional favorite at Walton-size dining tables. Its festive nature makes turkey an obvious crowd-pleaser at any big gathering. Today, however, the typical American household is just as likely to be only the two of you . . . or even just you! (Back in 1963, only 43 percent of U.S. households were made up of one or two people. That proportion rose to 50 percent by 1975, and it is still growing.)

Today's turkey is conveniently packaged in forms and quantities that suit America's changing life styles. In this section we've put together a selection of quick and easy recipes particularly suited to singles and couples, plus a collection of economical "large-quantity" dishes for big family gatherings. You'll find more crowd-pleasers in chapter 15.

Turkey Diane for One

1 teaspoon butter, margarine, or diet
    margarine
1 raw turkey breast slice (about 4
    ounces)
  Onion or garlic salt and pepper to
    taste
1 tablespoon white wine or water
1 generous dash of Worcestershire
    sauce
1 minced sprig fresh parsley (or
    pinch of parsley flakes)

Melt butter in a small nonstick skillet; rotate to spread evenly. Add turkey breast slice and brown over moderate flame, about 2 to 3 minutes each side. Remove to a heated plate and season with salt and pepper. Combine wine or water and Worcestershire sauce in skillet; stir over moderate heat until bubbling. Pour over turkey slice. Sprinkle with parsley.

Makes one serving, about 170 calories (155 calories with diet margarine). (Recipe may be doubled to serve two.)

Polynesian Sweet-and-Sour Turkey with Vegetables

1 turkey tenderloin (about 4 ounces)
1 cup frozen Oriental vegetables
2 teaspoons soy sauce
½ cup unsweetened pineapple juice
2 teaspoons lemon juice

Spray a nonstick skillet with cooking spray for no-fat frying. Brown turkey tenderloin quickly on each side; remove to a cutting board. Meanwhile, combine remaining ingredients in the skillet. Simmer, uncovered, until vegetables are tender and nearly all the juice has evaporated.

Meanwhile, cut the turkey into 1-inch cubes (they will be pink in the middle). Return diced turkey to the skillet. Cook, stirring, over low heat until the turkey is cooked through.

Makes one serving, about 250 calories. (Recipe may be doubled to serve two.)

Tarragon Turkey "Oven-Ragout"

1 turkey hindquarter (about 3½
    pounds)
4 medium peeled, quartered onions
1 pound scraped carrots, cut into 2
    in. lengths (or 1 bag frozen
    carrots)
2 cups tiny whole mushrooms
1½ cups dry white wine
1 teaspoon dried tarragon
  Salt and pepper to taste

Place hindquarter skin-side up in a nonstick Dutch oven or baking pan. Bake in preheated 450-degree oven 20 to 25 minutes, until skin is crisp. Drain and discard any fat.

Arrange vegetables under turkey. Add wine and sprinkle with seasonings. Lower heat to 325 degrees. Cover and bake until tender, about 1½ hours. Uncover during last 20 to 30 minutes.

Makes eight servings, about 470 calories each.

Leg of Turkey Meal-size Soup

1 turkey drumsick
2 cups water
1 peeled, thinly sliced onion
1 small bay leaf
   optional: ¼ teaspoon sage or
      poultry seasoning
   optional: ½ teaspoon MSG
1 cup sliced carrots (fresh or frozen)
1 cup thinly sliced celery
   Minced fresh parsley to taste
1 cup sliced fresh mushrooms
   Salt and pepper to taste

Note: It is not necessary to defrost turkey, if frozen.

In a soup kettle or pressure cooker, combine turkey drumstick with water, onion, and seasonings. Heat to boiling; then skim. Cover and simmer until meat is very tender, about 1½ hours (or 30 minutes in a pressure cooker, according to manufacturer's directions). Remove from heat.

Fill a 1-cup measure with ice cubes; then fill to the top with cold water. Pour into the pot to hasten cooling. When turkey is cool enough to handle, remove from broth. Separate meat and cut into bite-size chunks. Discard skin, tendons, and bones.

Skim fat from broth with bulb-type baster. Add carrots, celery, and parsley to broth. Cover and simmer until vegetables are tender. Add mushrooms; cover and simmer 2 minutes. Add turkey meat and heat through. Add salt and pepper to taste.

Makes three servings, about 295 calories each. (Recipe may be doubled to serve six.)

Italian Turkey-Vegetable Soup

1 turkey drumstick
2 cups tomato juice
1 peeled, thinly sliced onion
1 small minced clove garlic (or pinch
   of instant garlic)
½ teaspoon dried oregano or mixed
   Italian seasoning
1 cup sliced zucchini (fresh or
   frozen)
1 small seeded, diced green bell
   pepper
   optional: salt and pepper to taste
   Minced Italian parsley

Follow the recipe for Leg of Turkey Meal-size Soup (above), substituting tomato juice for the water. Omit MSG and add no salt unless needed.

Makes three servings, about 300 calories each.

Turkey Vegetable Chowder

1 turkey drumstick
¼ cup dry sherry
1¾ cups water
2 peeled, thinly sliced onions
optional: 1 small bay leaf
optional: pinch of ground nutmeg
optional: ½ teaspoon MSG
optional: ¼ teaspoon poultry
seasoning
1 cup sliced carrots (fresh or frozen)
½ cup sliced celery
⅔ cup sliced fresh mushrooms (or 1
2-ounce can, undrained)
1 cup skim milk
1½ tablespoons instant-blending flour
Salt and pepper to taste
1 tablespoon minced parsley

In a soup kettle or pressure cooker, combine turkey, wine, water, and onions (plus optional seasonings). Heat to boiling; then skim. Cover and simmer until turkey is tender, about 1½ hours (or 30 minutes in a pressure cooker, according to manufacturer's directions). Remove from heat.

Fill a 1-cup measure with ice cubes; then fill to the top with cold water. Pour into the pot to hasten cooling. When turkey is cool enough to handle, remove from broth. Separate meat and cut into bite-size chunks. Discard skin, tendons, and bones.

Skim fat from broth with bulb-type baster. Simmer carrots and celery in broth until tender; add mushrooms. Stir milk and flour together and stir into simmering broth until thick. Add diced turkey meat and heat through. Season to taste. Ladle into three bowls and sprinkle with parsley.

Makes three servings, about 345 calories each.

Turkeyburger with Wine Sauce

Pan-fry ¼-pound turkey patty in nonstick skillet with 1 teaspoon oil for about 4 minutes on each side for medium doneness. Sprinkle with salt and pepper. Remove patty from pan. Add 2 tablespoons dry red wine and stir to deglaze pan. Add a 4-ounce can of sliced mushrooms including liquid; simmer 2 minutes. Pour over turkeyburger.

About 280 calories each.

Turkey Sausage and Risotto for One

½ cup "instant" rice
½ cup boiling water
optional: few threads of saffron (or
pinch of turmeric)
Onion salt and pepper to taste
3 turkey sausage links
1 8-ounce can crushed tomatoes
Pinch of dried oregano or pizza
seasoning

Combine rice, boiling water, and saffron. Cover and set aside 5 minutes or more. Salt and pepper to taste.

Spray a nonstick skillet with cooking spray for no-fat frying. Brown the turkey sausages over high heat, turning to brown evenly. Pour off fat, if any. Stir in tomatoes and oregano. Cover and simmer 10 minutes. To serve, spoon over rice.

Makes one serving, about 393 calories. (Recipe may be doubled to serve two.)

Toaster-oven Turkey Ham and Pineapple for One

1 thick slice (4 ounces) turkey ham
1 juice-packed pineapple ring
2 tablespoons pineapple juice (from can)
Pinch of ground cloves, cinnamon, and mustard

Put turkey ham slice on baking tray of a toaster oven and top with pineapple. Combine remaining ingredients and pour over pineapple. Bake in toaster oven on highest setting just until heated through, about 5 minutes.

Makes one serving, about 200 calories.

Chinese Pepper Skillet for Two

1 peeled, halved, thinly sliced onion
2 seeded, halved green bell peppers, sliced into thin strips
1 small minced clove garlic (or pinch of instant garlic)
¾ cup (1 6-ounce can) tomato juice
1 tablespoon soy sauce
Pinch of powdered ginger
½ pound turkey bologna, cut into julienne strips

Combine all ingredients except turkey bologna in a nonstick skillet over moderate heat. Cover and simmer 2 minutes. Uncover and continue to simmer 4 to 5 minutes, stirring frequently, until vegetables are tender-crisp and most of the liquid has evaporated. Stir in sliced bologna at the last minute. Cook and stir until heated through.

Makes two servings, about 280 calories each. (Recipe may be doubled to serve four.)

Turkey Salami-Cheese Omelet

2 eggs (or ½ cup defrosted no-cholesterol substitute)
1 tablespoon skim milk
½ ounce turkey salami, cut into julienne strips
½ ounce shredded part-skim mozzarella or Swiss cheese
1 tablespoon minced fresh parsley
Salt and pepper to taste

Beat eggs and milk together. Spray an 8-inch nonstick omelet pan with cooking spray for no-fat frying. Heat over moderate flame. When hot, pour in eggs. Lift egg mixture with a spatula, to permit uncooked portion to run underneath. When egg mixture is set, pile turkey salami and cheese in the middle and sprinkle with parsley, salt, and pepper. Fold omelet over, enclosing the filling inside. Turn off heat. Cover pan with a heavy plate and leave undisturbed for a few minutes, until filling is warm. Turn omelet onto a plate and serve immediately.

In a hinged omelet pan: Divide egg mixture between two sides of the pan and cook. When set, put filling in one side and close the pan.

Makes one serving, about 240 calories with mozzarella; 250 calories with Swiss cheese (if using egg substitute, subtract 80 calories).

Turkey Salami and Peppers for One

1 seeded, sliced green bell pepper
½ cup tomato juice
   salt or garlic salt and pepper to
    taste
   Pinch of dried oregano or pizza
    seasoning
4 ounces diced turkey salami

Combine all ingredients except salami in a small nonstick skillet. Cover and simmer 4 minutes. Uncover and stir in salami. Cook, stirring, just until liquid evaporates into a thick sauce.

    Makes one serving, about 255 calories. (Recipe may be doubled to serve two.)

Cock-a-Doodle Curry

4 small peeled, quartered onions
2 trimmed, sliced ribs celery
1 seeded bell pepper (preferably
   red), cut into 1-inch cubes
1 cup fat-skimmed turkey broth
1 to 2 teaspoons curry powder (or to
   taste)
¼ teaspoon ground cinnamon or
   apple pie spice
1 cup sliced fresh mushrooms
¾ cup skim milk
2 tablespoons flour
1 cup (about 5 ounces) diced turkey
   pastrami

Combine vegetables with broth, curry powder, and cinnamon in a saucepan. Cover and simmer just until celery is tender-crisp (about 6 minutes). Stir in mushrooms and simmer, uncovered, 1 minute. Combine milk and flour in covered jar; shake until blended. Stir into simmering pot. Cook, stirring, until sauce is thick. Stir in pastrami and heat through. (Serve sprinkled with peanuts or raisins, if desired.)

    Makes two servings, about 275 calories each. (A total of 2 tablespoons of peanuts add 55 calories per serving; raisins 30 calories per serving.)

EIGHT ▶ TURKEY KID PLEASERS

ANYONE who's ever had one—or been one—knows that kids have a cuisine all their own, with rules that defy categorization. For example, everybody knows that kids don't care for spicy foods . . . and love chili and tacos. Kids don't like "mixtures" and "messy" foods . . . but they're crazy about pizza and spaghetti. And they don't like vegetables, or "foreign" foods. But their cafeteria favorite is chow mein. They get tired of the "same old thing" and hate to try anything new. One universal rule about kidfood: anything that's "good for you" is immediately suspect.

If you understand all this, today's turkey makes kid-pleasing easy. It's a good-for-you food that can be chili and spaghetti, or hot dogs and quarter pounders. Or a "baloney sandwich" or sausage pizza . . . or just plain turkey. Any way they like it, today's turkey is a nutritious alternative to the kinds of foods most kids are fond of.

Turkey Quarter Pounders

Divide a 1-pound package of ground turkey into quarters. Gently shape or pat each quarter into a round patty. Sprinkle with onion or garlic powder, if desired, or sprinkle with lemon juice, soy or Worcestershire sauce. Broil or barbecue 4 inches from heat source, 3 minutes per side. Or spray a nonstick skillet with cooking spray for no-fat frying. Cook 4 to 5 minutes each side, until cooked through. Turn gently with a spatula, without pressing down. (Serve on toasted hamburger buns with raw onions, ripe tomato slices, dill pickle chips; add catsup if desired.)

Each quarter pounder, about 210 calories (burger only).

"Special Sauce" for Turkeyburgers

Stir together equal parts regular or low-calorie Thousand Island dressing and catsup.

About 25 calories a tablespoon with low-calorie dressing, about 50 with regular dressing.

Turkey Cheeseburger

Divide ground turkey into "quarter pounders." Shape gently into patties. Broil 4 inches from heat source for 3 minutes; sprinkle with salt and pepper. Turn and broil 4 more minutes. Spread lightly with mustard (optional) and top each with a ½-ounce slice of sharp American or Cheddar cheese (or low-fat diet cheese). Place under broiler just until cheese is melted.

Each cheeseburger, about 315 calories with regular cheese; 245 with diet cheese; mustard adds 8 calories per teaspoon.

Turkey Pizzaburger Pronto

Broil a ¼-pound turkeyburger, 4 minutes each side. Top with one thin slice (½-ounce) part-skim mozzarella cheese, one tablespoon catsup, and a pinch of oregano. Return to broiler just until cheese is melted.

About 270 calories each.

Texas Turkeyburgers

1 pound ground turkey
Onion salt and pepper to taste
1 teaspoon chili powder (or more, to taste)

Combine turkey with remaining ingredients except tomato juice and cheese. Shape into four patties. Broil, turning once, and baste frequently with tomato juice. Slice cheese into four equal pieces. Top

4 tablespoons chopped green bell
  pepper (fresh or defrosted)
¾ cup (1 6-ounce can) tomato juice,
  regular or Bloody Mary-
  seasoned
2 ounces regular or diet American-
  style cheese

each burger with cheese and place under broiler just until the cheese begins to melt.

Makes four servings, about 280 calories each with regular cheese; about 245 calories with diet cheese.

Turkeyburger "Pizzarella"

1½ pounds ground turkey
1 egg (or 2 egg whites or ¼ cup
  defrosted no-cholesterol
  substitute)
  Garlic salt to taste
2 tablespoons dried onion flakes
1 8-ounce can tomato sauce
½ teaspoon dried oregano or mixed
  Italian seasoning
1 cup (4 ounces) shredded part-skim
  mozzarella or pizza cheese

Combine ground turkey, egg, garlic salt, onion flakes, 2 tablespoons of the tomato sauce, and seasoning. Toss lightly. In a nonstick 10-inch piepan, spread the turkey mixture to line the bottom and sides to form a crust. Bake in preheated 450-degree oven 10 to 12 minutes, until browned.

Remove from oven and pour on remaining tomato sauce. Sprinkle with cheese (and additional oregano, if desired.) Return to oven for an additional 5 to 7 minutes. To serve, cut into pizza-shaped wedges.

Makes six servings, about 290 calories each (285 calories each with egg whites or substitute).

Italian Turkey Sausage "Pie"

1 pound turkey breakfast sausage
1 egg
  Salt or garlic salt and pepper to
  taste
1 teaspoon dried oregano or mixed
  Italian seasoning
1 tablespoon olive oil
¾ cup (3 ounces) shredded part-skim
  mozzarella cheese

Toss sausage lightly with egg, salt, pepper, and oregano. Divide meat mixture into two equal parts. Add olive oil to a large nonstick skillet or electric frypan and rotate the skillet to spread. Put half the meat in the skillet and pat lightly to form 9- or 10-inch circle. Sprinkle on cheese. Cover cheese with remaining meat, patting lightly so cheese is completely covered and a thin, flat meatpie is formed. Turn heat to moderate. When bottom is well browned, cut into four pie-shaped wedges. With a spatula turn each wedge over carefully and continue cooking until bottom is well browned and cheese is melted. (Serve with heated tomato sauce, if desired.)

Makes four servings, about 330 calories each. (Each ½ cup plain tomato sauce adds about 30 calories.)

Speedy Skillet Spaghetti with Turkey Sausage

1 pound turkey sausage
1¼ cups fat-skimmed turkey broth
3½ cups water
1 6-ounce can tomato paste
    Garlic salt to taste
3 tablespoons minced onion (or 1
    tablespoon dried onion flakes)
1 teaspoon dried oregano
6 ounces (dry) very thin spaghetti,
    broken

Spread the sausage in a large, heavy nonstick skillet. Over moderate heat, brown slowly without adding fat, stirring constantly to avoid sticking. (Add a little water, if needed.) Add all remaining ingredients except spaghetti; heat to boiling. Add spaghetti, a little at a time. Cover and cook, stirring occasionally, until spaghetti is tender, about 10 minutes. Uncover and continue to simmer until sauce is thick. (Sprinkle with 6 teaspoons grated Parmesan cheese, if desired.)

Makes six servings, about 285 calories each; about 295 calories with cheese added.

Fruited Turkey Ham Kebabs

1 pound unsliced turkey ham
1 16-ounce can drained, juice-packed
    apricot halves
½ cup drained, juice-packed
    pineapple chunks
8 cherry tomatoes
½ cup defrosted, undiluted orange
    juice concentrate
1 teaspoon ground nutmeg

Cut turkey ham into 1-inch chunks. Use four large or eight small skewers to alternate turkey ham chunks, apricot halves, pineapple chunks, and cherry tomatoes, beginning and ending with turkey ham. Combine orange juice concentrate and nutmeg. Brush kebabs with orange-nutmeg glaze. Grill 6 to 8 inches from heat source until heated through, about 15 minutes. Brush with glaze frequently.

Makes four servings, about 300 calories each.

Baked Vegetable Casserole Bologna

1 peeled, diced eggplant
1 9-ounce package defrosted Italian
    green beans
1 16-ounce can undrained, chopped
    Italian plum tomatoes
1 pound diced turkey bologna
3 tablespoons grated extra-sharp
    Romano cheese
3 tablespoons Italian-seasoned bread
    crumbs

Combine vegetables and turkey bologna in oven-proof casserole. Sprinkle with cheese and crumbs. Bake at 375 degrees for 30 to 40 minutes.

Makes six servings, about 215 calories each.

Lean Wienies and Noodles

1 16-ounce can undrained, chopped tomatoes
2 cups water or fat-skimmed turkey broth
1 small peeled, minced onion (or 1 tablespoon instant onion)
1½ cups (dry) ruffle-edged noodles
8 turkey frankfurters, sliced into rounds
1 ounce chopped extra-sharp Cheddar cheese,
Salt and pepper to taste

Combine tomatoes, water, and onion in a nonstick saucepan and heat to boiling. Stir in noodles a few at a time. Lower heat and simmer, covered, 10 minutes, stirring occasionally, until noodles are nearly tender. Add turkey franks. Simmer, uncovered, until nearly all the liquid has evaporated. Remove from heat and stir in cheese. Season to taste.

Makes four main-course servings, about 365 calories each (with broth 380 calories each).

Quick Turkey Devil Dogs

2 tablespoons butter, margarine, or diet margarine
2 teaspoons prepared mustard
2 teaspoons chili powder
Seasoned salt to taste
1 pound (10) turkey franks
10 toasted hot dog buns

Melt butter in square baking pan. Stir in mustard, chili powder, and salt. Have franks at room temperature. Place in pan and shake pan until all franks are coated with mixture. Place pan under broiler for 4 to 5 minutes until franks are hot. Serve on buns.

Makes ten servings, about 240 calories each (230 calories each with diet margarine).

Skewered Turkey Franks and Apples

1 pound (10) turkey frankfurters
6 unpeeled red apples
1 teaspoon salad oil

Slice franks into 2-inch lengths. Use an apple sectioner or sharp knife to core and cut each apple into six wedges. Alternate franks and apples on skewers. Brush lightly with oil.

Broil or barbecue 3 inches from heat source, turning once, just until franks are crisp and apples are still firm.

Makes six servings, about 265 calories each.

NINE ▶ TURKEY ENCORES

"LEFTOVER" is a sad sort of wallflower word with a connotation just a shade better than "reject." True "leftovers" just shouldn't happen! Because they mean that the food either wasn't very good, or that you made too much to begin with. Setting out more food than people really need is worse than wasteful, because it promotes overeating.

However, food that's left over with a plan in mind is something else. We prefer to call that food "planned-overs" or "energy savers." Double-batch cooking that saves you from making dinner another night saves *your* energy as well as the utility company's. Cooked foods that can be recycled into a different dish tomorrow (or next week, from the freezer) save steps as well as time.

Versatile turkey is a prime choice for snappy comebacks. In this section, we've included recipes that start with turkey that's already cooked.

Turkey and Mushrooms à la Reine

½ pound sliced fresh mushrooms
1 tablespoon butter, margarine, or diet margarine
½ cup sherry
4 tablespoons peeled, minced onion

Place mushrooms in a nonstick skillet with butter and 3 tablespoons wine. Cook, stirring, over moderate heat until wine evaporates and mushrooms brown. Add remaining wine, onions, nutmeg, and turkey. Simmer 1 minute.

¼ teaspoon nutmeg
2 cups (about 10 ounces) cubed
   cooked turkey
2 cups skim milk
4 tablespoons flour
6 tablespoons grated Parmesan
   cheese
Salt and pepper to taste
2 tablespoons minced fresh parsley

Combine milk and flour. Stir into skillet over low heat until sauce thickens and bubbles. Stir in Parmesan; cook, stirring, until melted. Salt and pepper to taste. Stir in parsley. (Sprinkle with paprika, and spoon over toast points, rice, or noodles, if desired.)

Makes four servings, about 265 calories each (255 with diet margarine). (Each toast point adds about 50 calories with low-calorie bread; about 65 calories with regular bread. Each ½ cup tender-cooked noodles or fluffy rice adds about 100 calories.)

Turkey-Spaghetti Dinner Pronto

1¼ cups fat-skimmed turkey or
   chicken broth
1 6-ounce can tomato paste
   optional: 1 or 2 tablespoons dry
   red wine
1 tablespoon instant onion
   optional: pinch of instant garlic
1 teaspoon dried oregano or mixed
   Italian seasoning
Salt and pepper to taste
2 cups (about 10 ounces) diced
   cooked turkey
4 cups tender-cooked spaghetti

In a saucepan combine turkey broth, tomato paste, and wine. Add seasonings. Cover and simmer 5 minutes. Stir in turkey until heated through. Serve over hot, drained spaghetti.

Makes four servings, about 330 calories each.

Turkey Chili with Rice

3 cups (about 1 pound) cooked
   minced turkey meat (from
   turkey necks)
2 ribs celery chopped
1 peeled, chopped onion
1 chopped green bell pepper
Garlic salt to taste
3 cups fat-skimmed turkey broth
1 16-ounce can chopped tomatoes
1 cup raw rice
1 6-ounce can tomato paste
2 teaspoons chili powder
1 teaspoon prepared mustard

Combine ingredients in a sauce pan. Cover and simmer, stirring occasionally, until rice is tender, about 35 minutes.

Makes six servings, about 320 calories each.

Turkey and Zucchini Pronto

1¼ cups fat-skimmed turkey or
    chicken broth
1 6-ounce can tomato paste
2 medium sliced zucchini
1 peeled, minced onion (or 3
    tablespoons instant dried
    onion)
    optional: 1 minced clove gralic (or
    ⅛ teaspoon instant garlic)
1 teaspoon dried basil or mixed
    Italian seasoning
2 cups (about 10 ounces) diced
    cooked turkey
4 tablespoons grated extra-sharp
    Romano cheese

Combine all ingredients except turkey and cheese in a large nonstick skillet. Simmer uncovered, stirring frequently, until most of the liquid has evaporated (10 to 12 minutes). Stir in turkey and heat through. Sprinkle with cheese and serve immediately.

Makes four servings, about 225 calories each.

Illustrations on following pages:

(A) Turkey Breakfast Ham Slices (*recipe on p. 149*)

(B) Turkey Cantonese (*recipe on p. 33*)

(C) Turkey Parmigiana (*recipe on p. 33*)

(D) Barbecued Cut-up Turkey Parts (*see p. 96*)

(E) Turkey Franks 'n' Sauerkraut (*recipe on p. 76*)

(F) Turkey Hors d'Oeuvres: Pastrami and Bologna Pinwheels (*recipe on p. 165*); Nut Balls (*p. 163*)

(G) Turkey Ham and Spinach Salad (*recipe on p. 142*); Greek Pita Pockets (*p. 154*)

(H) Rolled Turkey Thighs with Cherries (*recipe on p. 54*)

Turkey Aloha

2 pounds roast turkey, cut into julienne strips
2 tablespoons cornstarch
1 tablespoon soy sauce
1 16-ounce can drained, unsweetened pineapple chunks (reserve juice)
¼ cup tomato juice
1 8½-ounce can drained, sliced water chestnuts
1 7-ounce package partially thawed pea pods
16 halved cherry tomatoes

In a large nonstick skillet combine turkey, cornstarch, soy sauce, pineapple juice, and tomato juice. Cook, stirring, over medium heat, until mixture simmers and thickens. Stir in pineapple chunks and water chestnuts. Cook over low heat 3 minutes. Add pea pods and cook 2 minutes longer. Remove from heat and fold in tomatoes.

Makes eight servings, about 295 calories each.

Main-Course Skillet Chowder

1 tablespoon butter or margarine
2 tablespoons water
1 large peeled, halved, thinly sliced onion
2 cups fat-skimmed turkey broth
2 peeled, cubed potatoes
2 scraped, thinly sliced carrots
1 thinly sliced rib celery
2 cups skim milk
2 tablespoons flour
Salt and white pepper to taste
2 cups (about 10 ounces) diced cooked white meat turkey
2 tablespoons minced fresh parsley
optional: paprika to taste

Combine butter and water in a large nonstick skillet or electric frypan. Heat until butter melts. Spread onion in a shallow layer. Cover and simmer 1 minute. Uncover and continue to cook until liquid evaporates and onions are soft. Add broth, potatoes, carrots, and celery. Cover and simmer over low heat just until potatoes are tender.

Combine milk and flour in a large covered jar and shake until blended. Gently stir into simmering skillet. Salt and pepper to taste. Cook, stirring until mixture simmers and thickens slightly. Add diced turkey; simmer 5 minutes more. Sprinkle with parsley and paprika to taste.

Makes four servings, about 310 calories each.

Turkey and Broccoli Primavera

1 cup fat-skimmed turkey broth
1 10-ounce package defrosted cut
    broccoli
1 large peeled, chopped onion
1 minced clove garlic (or ⅛ teaspoon
    instant garlic)
½ teaspoon dried oregano
⅛ teaspoon ground nutmeg
⅔ cup skim milk
1 tablespoon flour
1 cup (about 5 ounces) diced cooked
    turkey breast
  Salt and pepper to taste
3 cups tender-cooked spaghetti
3 tablespoons grated Parmesan
    cheese

Heat broth to boiling in a nonstick skillet or electric frypan over high heat. Add broccoli, onion, garlic, oregano, and nutmeg. Cook, uncovered, stirring frequently, until nearly all the liquid evaporates. Combine milk and flour in a covered jar and shake until blended. Pour into simmering skillet over low heat, stirring until sauce thickens. Add diced turkey and simmer 2 minutes. Salt and pepper to taste. Spoon over hot, drained pasta; sprinkle with cheese.

    Makes three servings, about 360 calories each.

One-pan Turkey Cacciatore

1¼ cups fat-skimmed turkey or
    chicken broth (homemade or
    canned)
¼ cup dry sherry or other white wine
    or water
1 cup water
1 6-ounce can tomato paste
1 seeded, diced green bell pepper
1 peeled, chopped onion (or 2
    tablespoons dried onion)
1 teaspoon dried oregano
6 ounces (dry) ruffle-edged noodles
2 cups (about 10 ounces) diced oven-
    roasted turkey

Combine all ingredients except noodles and turkey in a covered pot. Heat to boiling. Stir in noodles a little at a time. Cover and simmer 20 minutes, stirring frequently. Uncover and add turkey. Continue to simmer, uncovered, until most of the liquid is evaporated

    Makes four servings, about 330 calories each.

TEN ▶ TAKING STOCK WITH TURKEY

TEN REASONS to be a super soup maker:

▶ Soup can be the ideal no-work meal. Homemade meal-size soups go straight from the freezer to the saucepan to the soup bowl, with a minimum of fuss.

▶ Soup is ideal for calorie counters. All the fat (and all the fat *calories*) floats to the surface where you can whisk it away!

▶ Soup can be plain or fancy, everyday or exotic: turkey noodle or Turkey Sopa de Tortilla.

▶ Soup can be a snack or an appetizer or a whole meal, a light lunch or a hearty dinner.

▶ Soup as a first course is actually a "de-appetizer" that takes the edge off your appetite and minimizes overeating. That's good news for waistline watchers!

▶ Soup is a great place to "hide" vegetables for greenery-shy youngsters. Even kids who "don't like vegetables" enjoy them in soup. With blender-puréed soups you can even make vegetables "disappear."

▶ Soup travels well. You can brown-bag hot soups in a Thermos for desktop lunches or carry frozen soups to your vacation place for on-the-spot warm-ups.

► Soup is something everybody likes: tots and teenagers, construction workers and career girls, farm folks and city-dwellers. And soup is something everybody can enjoy—babies, convalescents, those on special diets, and especially those who have to count calories!

► Soup is good for you! Studies show that there's something to "Grandma's penicillin," after all! The steamy vapors, the spices and seasonings are just what the doctor ordered for stuffy noses!

► Soup is adaptable, equally suited for crowds, couples, or singles. What easier way to entertain good friends than to serve a hearty meal-size soup from a big tureen while everyone sits by the fire? What's simpler than nourishing knife-and-fork soup when you're dining alone?

In this section we show you how to make fat-free turkey stock and how to use it in soups and as seasoning for a selection of vegetable dishes.

Homemade Turkey Soup Base

5 turkey necks (or 4 turkey wing portions [about 2½ pounds] or a meaty turkey frame from whole roast turkey)
3 quarts water
1 to 2 tablespoons salt

OPTIONAL SEASONING INGREDIENTS
2 teaspoons MSG
1 peeled, quartered onion
2 sliced ribs celery
1 scraped, sliced carrot
1 or 2 cloves garlic
1 bay leaf

Combine turkey, water, and salt in a soup kettle (or pressure cooker) and heat to boiling. Skim foam. Add optional ingredients. Cover and simmer until turkey is very tender, about 2 hours (or 45 minutes in a pressure cooker, according to manufacturer's directions). Remove turkey from broth and set aside until cool enough to handle. Strain broth and discard seasoning residue. Chill strained broth until fat rises to surface and can be removed. When turkey is cool enough to handle, separate the meat. Discard skin and bones.

Pour fat-skimmed broth into covered jars and store in refrigerator. Or label the jars and freeze. (Don't fill jars to the top; allow 1-inch headroom for expansion.)

Package meat in meal-size portions. Wrap, label, and freeze.

Each cup of fat-skimmed turkey broth, about 50 calories; each cup of diced cooked turkey meat (5 ounces), about 265 calories.

Homemade Frozen Turkey Bouillon Cubes

Simmer fat-skimmed turkey broth, uncovered, until reduced by half. Allow to cool. Pour into ice cube trays and freeze firm. Remove cubes from trays and pack cubes in plastic bags. Label and store in the freezer. To reconstitute 1 cup broth, combine ½ cup water and about 5 cubes in a saucepan and heat until cubes melt and simmer. Or add 1 or 2 frozen turkey cubes to the water in which vegetables are cooked for flavor (no butter needed!).

Basic Turkey-Vegetable Soup for Four

4 cups fat-skimmed turkey broth or
    homemade turkey soup base
    (p. 126)
1 cup water
1 peeled, sliced onion
2 scraped, sliced carrots
2 sliced ribs celery
  Salt and pepper to taste
2 cups (about 5 ounces) diced
    cooked turkey meat

Combine all ingredients except turkey. Cover and simmer until vegetables are tender, about 20 minutes. Add turkey and heat through.

Makes four meal-size servings, about 185 calories each.

Manhattan Turkey Chowder

1 16-ounce can undrained tomatoes
4 chopped ribs celery
3 peeled, diced potatoes
3 scraped, diced carrots
½ teaspoon poultry seasoning
  Salt and pepper to taste
2 cups fat-skimmed turkey broth
2 cups water
3 cups (about 1 pound) diced turkey
    pastrami

Combine all ingredients except turkey pastrami in a large saucepan. Cover and cook gently over low heat 1 hour. Add turkey pastrami and heat through.

Makes eight servings, about 135 calories each.

New England Turkey Chowder

¾ cup peeled, chopped onion
1 tablespoon butter, margarine, or
    diet margarine
2 cups peeled, cubed potatoes
    Salt and pepper to taste
1 cup water
2 cups (about 10 ounces) diced
    turkey ham
1 cup evaporated skim milk

Sauté onion in butter in a large saucepan. Add potatoes, salt, pepper, and water. Simmer 20 minutes. Mix in turkey ham and milk. Heat gently, but do not boil.

Makes six servings, about 165 calories each (160 calories each with diet margarine).

Cream of Turkey Soup

2 cups (about 10 ounces) cubed
    oven-roasted turkey breast
    fillet
1 cup finely diced celery
¼ cup peeled, minced onion
1 cup grated carrot
2 tablespoons chopped fresh parsley
2 cups fat-skimmed turkey broth
    Salt and pepper to taste
    optional: 1 teaspoon MSG
2 cups skim milk
¼ cup flour

In a large saucepan combine all ingredients except milk and flour. Cover and simmer 10 to 15 minutes. Combine milk and flour in a covered jar. Shake well to combine. Stir into soup. Cover and simmer over very low heat, stirring frequently, an additional 5 minutes.

Makes six servings, about 155 calories each.

Creamy Turkey Soup

2 turkey drumsticks
2 quarts water
1 teaspoons salt (or to taste)
    optional: 2 peeled onions, 2 ribs
    celery, 2 small bay leaves, and
    1 teaspoon MSG
2 cups skim milk
⅓ cup flour
    Fresh parsley for garnish

Cover drumsticks with water. Add salt (and optional ingredients). Cook, covered, over moderate heat for 1 to 1½ hours, or until tender.

Strain broth; let drumsticks cool. Set aside broth until any fat rises to surface. Skim fat with a bulb-type baster. Heat strained, fat-skimmed broth to boiling. Stir milk and flour together. Stir into broth, until simmering.

Meanwhile, remove meat from drumsticks and cut into bite-size pieces. Discard skin, tendons and bones. Stir meat into simmering soup until heated through. Garnish with parsley.

Makes eight meal-size servings, about 225 calories each; with optional ingredients 235 calories each.

Turkey Bisque

2 cups fat-skimmed turkey broth
¼ cup dry white wine
2 cups skim milk
2 tablespoons instant-blending flour
  Onion salt and pepper to taste
  Pinch of nutmeg
  Paprika
  Few minced sprigs fresh parsley

In a saucepan combine broth and wine. Simmer down to about 1 cupful. Stir cold milk and flour together and gradually stir into the simmering broth. Cook, stirring, over low heat until thick and bubbling. Season to taste. Sprinkle with paprika and parsley.

Makes four servings, about 75 calories each.

Main-Course Bisque for Two

Follow recipe for Turkey Bisque (above).

After seasoning soup, stir in 1 cup (about 5 ounces) diced or shredded cooked turkey; heat through.

Makes two main-course servings, about 185 calories each.

Hearty Turkey Soup

 5 turkey necks
 2 quarts water
 7 bay leaves
 1 teaspoon celery salt
10 peppercorns
 2 cups peeled, chopped onions
 2 cups chopped celery
 2 tablespoons raw rice
 1 cup scraped, diced carrots
   optional: ¼ cup thinly sliced green
     onion
 2 tablespoons soy sauce

Place necks in soup kettle with water. Add bay leaves, celery salt, and pepper. Bring to boil and skim. Simmer 1½ hours.

Remove necks and allow to cool; skim fat from broth. Add onions, celery, rice, and carrots. Cover and simmer 20 to 25 minutes.

Meanwhile, remove meat from necks and discard bones. Combine meat with soup and heat through. Add green onions and soy sauce.

Makes six servings, about 360 calories each (370 calories each with green onion).

French Turkey-Carrot Potage

1 pound scraped, thinly sliced carrots
1 small peeled, chopped onion
2 thinly sliced ribs celery
3 cups fat-skimmed turkey broth
Pinch of thyme
1 bay leaf
  optional: 2 tablespoons dry sherry
¼ cup raw rice
2 cups (about 10 ounces) diced cooked turkey meat (from drumsticks)

Combine all ingredients except turkey meat in covered saucepan. Simmer until carrots are tender (about 20 minutes). Remove bay leaf; add turkey. Heat through.

Makes four servings, about 190 calories each.

Turkey Gumbo

5 turkey necks
2 tablespoons flour
4 cups water
1 cup peeled, chopped onions
2 cups okra (fresh or frozen)
2 cups seeded, chopped ripe tomatoes (or 1 16-ounce can, chopped)
1 cup diced celery
2 tablespoons chopped fresh parsley
  optional: 1 minced clove garlic
⅓ cup raw rice
Salt and pepper to taste

Cut turkey necks in serving-size portions. Dredge lightly with flour. Arrange on a nonstick tray and bake in preheated 450-degree oven 20 to 25 minutes, turning once, until skin is crisp.

Combine turkey necks with remaining ingredients in a soup pot. Cover and simmer until tender, 30 minutes or more.

Makes five servings, about 495 calories each.

Mexican Turkey Vegetable Soup

2½ cups fat-skimmed turkey broth
1 8-ounce can undrained tomatoes
2 peeled, chopped onions
2 thinly sliced ribs celery
1 seeded, diced green bell pepper
1 minced clove garlic
½ cup frozen cut corn
1½ teaspoons dried oregano
1 teaspoon ground cumin

Combine all ingredients except turkey in a soup kettle. Cover and simmer 20 minutes. Add turkey and heat through.

Makes four lunch- or supper-size servings, about 210 calories each.

Salt, pepper, and hot pepper to taste
2 cups (about 10 ounces) diced cooked turkey

Italian Eggplant and Turkey Meatball Soup

½ pound ground turkey or turkey breakfast sausage
1 peeled, minced onion
1 small peeled, diced eggplant
2 sliced ribs celery
1 16-ounce can undrained, chopped Italian tomatoes
2 cups fat-skimmed turkey broth
4 tablespoons (dry) protein-enriched elbow macaroni
  optional: 1 minced clove garlic
1 teaspoon dried oregano or basil
2 tablespoons minced fresh parsley
  Salt and pepper to taste
4 tablespoons grated extra-sharp Romano cheese

Use a melon baller to shape turkey into tiny balls. Place under the broiler to brown (or brown in a large nonstick skillet that has been sprayed with cooking spray for no-stick frying). Combine browned meatballs with remaining ingredients except cheese. Cover and simmer 25 to 30 minutes. Spoon into four soup bowls and sprinkle with cheese.

Makes four meal-size servings, about 245 calories each.

Spanish Turkey Soup with Zucchini

1 16-ounce can tomatoes
2 cups (about 10 ounces) diced smoked or cooked turkey
1 peeled, chopped onion
1 minced clove garlic (or pinch of instant garlic)
1 bay leaf
1 cup tomato juice
1 cup fat-skimmed turkey or chicken broth
1 teaspoon lemon juice
  optional: ¼ teaspoon dried basil or oregano
  Salt and pepper to taste
1 small sliced zucchini (or 1 10-ounce package defrosted zucchini)

Break up tomatoes with a fork. In a saucepan combine all ingredients except zucchini. Cover and simmer 30 minutes. Stir in zucchini and simmer an additional 5 minutes. Serve hot.

Makes four servings, about 145 calories each with smoked turkey; 195 calories each with regular cooked turkey.

Turkey Cock-a-Leekie

2 young turkey wings
4 cups water
  Salt to taste
  optional: ½ teaspoon MSG
4 cups sliced leeks (or 4 peeled,
    sliced onions)
18 pitted prunes
12 peppercorns

Place turkey wings in a large pot with water to cover; add salt and optional MSG. Simmer, covered, about 1 hour, or until turkey is tender.

Remove turkey; set aside to cool. Skim broth of any fat.

Slice the white part of the leeks; add to the broth; add prunes and peppercorns. Cover, and simmer 20 minutes.

Meanwhile, skin and bone wings; dice meat. Discard bones and skin. Add meat to soup and heat through.

Makes six main-dish servings, about 350 calories each.

Turkey Mulligatawny Soup

1 turkey thigh
  Paprika
1½ cups (1 12-ounce can) tomato
    juice
4 cups water
1 bay leaf
⅛ teaspoon nutmeg
2 teaspoons curry powder (or more,
    to taste)
2 scraped, thinly sliced carrots
2 peeled, halved, thinly sliced onions
2 thickly sliced ribs celery
4 tablespoons chopped fresh parsley
4 tablespoons raw rice
2 unpeeled, cored, diced red apples

Spray a large nonstick skillet with cooking spray for no-fat frying. Brown the turkey thigh skin-side down, until skin is crisp and well rendered of fat. Turn to brown evenly. Drain and discard any fat. Turn turkey skin-side up and sprinkle with paprika. Add tomato juice, water, bay leaf, nutmeg, and curry. Cover and simmer until turkey is tender, 1 hour or more.

Bone turkey and cut meat in cubes. Skim fat from surface of broth. Add remaining ingredients except apples and simmer until rice is tender, about 20 minutes. Add diced apples and heat through. Serve in large shallow soup plates with knife, fork, and soup spoon.

Makes five main-course servings, about 380 calories each.

Turkey-Vegetable Soup Laredo

2 turkey wings
4 cups water
  Salt and pepper to taste
  optional: ½ teaspoon MSG

Combine turkey wings, water, salt, and pepper in soup kettle. Cover and simmer 1 hour or more, until meat falls from bones. Strain liquid into bowl and chill until fat rises to the surface and hardens.

1 scraped, thinly sliced carrot
2 ribs celery, cut into 2-inch lengths
1 peeled, chopped onion
1 peeled, chopped clove garlic
½ small diced red or green bell
   pepper
2 tablespoons raw rice
2 tablespoons chopped fresh parsley
  Pinch of oregano and ground
   cumin
1 to 2 teaspoons of chili powder to
   taste

Remove and discard fat. Remove turkey meat from bones and dice. Discard skin and bones.

Combine fat-skimmed broth with remaining ingredients in soup kettle. Simmer until vegetables are tender, about 20 to 30 minutes. Add turkey meat and heat through.

Makes six servings, about 320 calories each.

Turkey Sopa de Tortilla (Turkey Tortilla Soup)

2½ cups fat-skimmed turkey or
    chicken broth (homemade or
    canned)
2 cups (about 10 ounces) diced
   cooked turkey meat
2 peeled, halved, thinly sliced onions
2 seeded, diced red or green bell
   peppers (or 1 of each)
2 peeled, diced ripe tomatoes (or 1 8-
   ounce can, chopped)
1 teaspoon chili powder (or to taste)
½ teaspoon dried oregano
8 cheese-flavored tortilla chips,
   broken up
4 tablespoons shredded extra-sharp
   Cheddar or American cheese

In a saucepan combine all ingredients except tortilla chips and cheese. Cover and simmer 8 to 10 minutes, or until vegetables are tender. Garnish with chips and cheese.

Makes four servings, about 245 calories each.

Meal-Size French Turkey-Onion Soup

1 10-ounce can undiluted French
   onion soup
1 8-ounce can undrained, sliced
   carrots
1 cup water
1 cup (about 5 ounces) diced cooked
   dark-meat or white-meat
   turkey
2 ounces shredded Swiss cheese

In a saucepan combine soup, carrots, and water, and heat to boiling. Simmer 2 minutes. Add diced turkey to soup; simmer until heated through. Spoon into 2 ovenproof bowls. Top each with cheese. Place bowls under broiler just until cheese is melted.

Makes two servings, about 375 calories each.

No-Butter-Needed Frozen Vegetables

1 10-ounce package frozen
    vegetables
½ to ¾ cup fat-skimmed turkey broth
    optional: 1 tablespoon peeled,
      minced onion (or 1 teaspoon
      dried onion)
Salt or seasoned salt and pepper to
    taste

Note: This recipe works well for almost any frozen vegetable.

Spread the frozen vegetables in a nonstick skillet or (electric) frypan. Add ½ cup broth and remaining ingredients; simmer over low heat, stirring to separate, until vegetables are tender-crisp and liquid evaporates. (Add more broth, if needed.) Do not cover. Green vegetables will be bright green, and the flavor of all vegetables will be fresh.

Makes three servings, about 70 calories each.

Green Beans Amandine

2 tablespoons slivered or sliced
    almonds
1 10-ounce package frozen whole
    green beans
½ cup fat-skimmed turkey broth
Salt and pepper

Spread almonds in a small skillet; shake skillet over moderate heat, adding no oil. Cook until nuts are toasted. (Watch carefully and do not allow them to blacken or burn.) Remove almonds from skillet and set aside.

Combine green beans and broth in the skillet. Cook, stirring, until all the broth has evaporated. Toss with almonds, salt, and pepper to taste (no butter needed!).

Makes three servings, about 70 calories each.

Frozen Broccoli "Stir-Fried" Without Oil

1 10-ounce package partly defrosted
    broccoli spears
½ peeled, chopped onion
½ cup fat-skimmed turkey broth
    optional: 2 tablespoons diced red
      bell pepper
1 tablespoon soy sauce

Use a serrated knife to cut the block of broccoli in thirds (so that each spear is divided into three pieces). Combine all ingredients except optional pepper and soy sauce in a nonstick skillet. Cook, uncovered, stirring, over low heat until nearly all the liquid evaporates. Stir in pepper and soy sauce at the last minute.

Makes three servings, about 45 calories each.

Scalloped Broccoli

1 10-ounce package frozen cut
    broccoli
½ cup fat-skimmed turkey broth
1 tablespoon peeled, minced onion
    (or 1 teaspoon dried onion)
    Salt and pepper to taste
3 tablespoons low-fat mayonnaise

In a saucepan, combine frozen broccoli, broth, onion; add salt and pepper to taste. Cover and cook until broccoli can be broken up. Uncover and cook until tender; do not drain. Stir in mayonnaise. Cook, stirring, over low heat until liquid is evaporated.

Makes three servings, about 55 calories each.

Carrots in Wine Sauce

3 cups scraped, sliced fresh carrots
    (or 1 20-ounce bag, frozen)
1 cup fat-skimmed turkey broth
¼ cup dry white wine
2 peeled, chopped onions
    Salt and pepper to taste
    optional: pinch of ground
    cinnamon
4 teaspoons cornstarch
¼ cup cold water

In a saucepan combine all ingredients except cornstarch and water. Cover and simmer just until carrots are tender, about 10 minutes or about 5 minutes if frozen. Mix cornstarch and cold water together and stir into saucepan. Cook, stirring, over low heat until sauce is thick. (Sprinkle with chopped fresh parsley, if desired.)

Makes six servings, about 55 calories each.

French Carrot Compote

2 cups scraped, sliced carrots (fresh
    or frozen)
3 thinly sliced ribs celery
1 small peeled, halved, thinly sliced
    onion
¼ pound sliced fresh mushrooms (or
    1 4-ounce can, undrained)
1 cup fat-skimmed turkey broth
¼ teaspoon dried rosemary
    Salt and pepper to taste
1½ teaspoons cornstarch

In a saucepan combine vegetables with ¾ cup broth. Add seasonings. Cover and simmer 10 to 12 minutes, until vegetables are tender. Combine cornstarch with remaining ¼ cup broth. Add to vegetables, stirring until sauce simmers and thickens.

Makes six servings, about 35 calories each.

Cauliflower au Gratin

4 cups fresh cauliflower buds (or 2 10-ounce packages or 1 20-ounce bag, frozen)
¾ cup fat-skimmed turkey broth
  Salt or seasoned salt to taste
¾ cup skim milk
3 tablespoons flour
½ cup shredded sharp American or Cheddar cheese
  optional: 2 tablespoons unseasoned bread crumbs
  Paprika

Combine cauliflower and broth in a heavy saucepan. Salt to taste. Cover closely and simmer just until tender, about 10 minutes (or about 5 minutes if frozen). Do not drain.

In a covered jar shake milk and flour together to blend well, then add to saucepan. Shake the pan gently to mix well. Simmer, shaking the pan occasionally, until sauce simmers and thickens. Spoon the cauliflower into a shallow oven-proof casserole. Sprinkle with cheese, optional bread crumbs, and paprika. Broil until topping is golden and bubbling.

Makes eight servings, about 65 calories each (70 calories each with bread crumbs).

Golden Curried Rice

3 cups fat-skimmed turkey broth (homemade or canned)
1 large peeled, minced onion
3 minced ribs celery
  Salt or garlic salt and pepper to taste
1 teaspoon turmeric
1 teaspoon curry powder (or more to taste)
3½ cups raw "instant" rice
1 6-ounce can defrosted orange juice concentrate
2 peeled, diced eating oranges
  optional: 1 tablespoon shredded orange peel
⅔ cup golden raisins

In a saucepan combine broth, onion, celery, and seasonings. Cover and simmer 10 minutes. Add rice and heat to boiling. Then add orange juice concentrate, diced oranges, peel, if desired, and raisins. Cook, stirring, over low heat just until heated through. Cover tightly and set aside 5 to 10 minutes, until liquid is absorbed. Fluff with a fork before serving.

Makes sixteen servings, about 150 calories each.

Turkey Rice

2 finely minced ribs celery
1 peeled, minced onion
1 cup fat-skimmed turkey broth
1 cup dry "instant" rice
  Salt or seasoned salt and pepper to taste

In a saucepan combine celery, onion, and broth. Cover and simmer 10 minutes. Stir in rice. Cover and set aside about 5 minutes, until liquid is absorbed. Fluff with a fork before serving. Season to taste.

Makes four servings, about 125 calories each. (Recipe may be doubled or tripled.)

Italian Skillet Zucchini

1 10-ounce package defrosted sliced
   green zucchini
1 teaspoon olive oil
⅓ cup fat-skimmed turkey broth
   optional: 1 small minced clove
       garlic (or pinch of instant
       garlic)
   optional: ¼ teaspoon dried
       oregano or mixed Italian
       seasoning
Salt and pepper to taste

Arrange zucchini in single layer in a nonstick skillet. Add remaining ingredients. Cook, stirring, over low heat until all the liquid evaporates and zucchini slices just begin to brown in remaining oil.

Makes three servings, under 40 calories each.

ELEVEN ▸ TURKEY IN THE SALAD

PURISTS used to argue over whether the salad should be eaten before the meal or after. Today, more than likely, salad *is* the meal! In case you haven't noticed, salad meals are *in*!

And nutrition watchers couldn't be happier. Mother Nature's greens are important to a well-balanced diet—fat-free, low in calories, high in appetite-appeasing bulk and fiber.

All it takes to turn a salad into a whole meal is the addition of a protein-rich food. But if the protein food is high in fat—like hard cheese or greasy "cold cuts"—the calorie-saving advantage of salad meals will be lost. That's where today's turkey comes in. Ready-to-eat turkey products, diced into bite-size cubes or sliced into thin julienne strips, can turn any favorite vegetable combination into a full-size, nutrition-wise, no-cook lunch or dinner. Turkey deli meats—turkey ham, pastrami, salami, and bologna—can serve as a stand-in for the high-fat cold meats usually used in salad bowls. Ready-to-eat smoked turkey can be sliced or diced to add savory flavor to any favorite vegetable or fruit combination. The availability of low-fat, low-calorie bottled salad dressings in all your favorite types make slim salad meals extra easy. Here are some ideas:

138

Marinated Orchard Salad

DRESSING
¼ cup orange juice
¼ cup regular or low-calorie Italian
   salad dressing
1½ teaspoons minced fresh parsley
1⅓ cups peeled, cubed orange
1⅓ cups unpeeled, cubed red apples
1 cup cubed zucchini
2½ cups (about 12½ ounces) cubed
   oven-roasted turkey

Toss dressing with fruit, vegetables, and turkey. Let marinate in the refrigerator 1 hour before serving.

Makes six lunch-size servings, about 200 calories each with regular salad dressing; about 150 calories each with low-calorie dressings.

Turkey Waldorf Salad

4 diced ribs celery
2 small unpeeled, cored, diced red
   apples
2 cups diced oven-roasted turkey
2 tablespoons low-fat mayonnaise
2 tablespoons plain low-fat yogurt
Salt and pepper to taste
Lettuce

Mix all ingredients and chill. Serve on lettuce.

Makes four meal-size servings, about 160 calories each.

Turkey Mac Salad

1½ cups tender-cooked macaroni
¼ cup low-fat mayonnaise
¼ cup plain low-fat yogurt
1½ tablespoons lemon juice
   Celery salt and pepper to taste
½ pound diced oven-roasted turkey
   breast
½ cup seeded, chopped green bell
   pepper
2 tablespoons chopped green onion
½ cup chopped ripe tomatoes
½ cup defrosted frozen peas

As soon as macaroni is cooked, rinse with cold water and drain. Toss with mayonnaise, yogurt, lemon juice, salt, and pepper.

Stir in turkey and vegetables. Stir carefully until entire salad is coated. Chill to blend flavors.

Makes six servings, about 140 calories each.

Turkey Salad Vinaigrette

¾ pound diced oven-roasted turkey
    breast
2 cups cooked rice
2 cups defrosted frozen mixed
    vegetables
5 tablespoons white-wine vinegar
2 tablespoons oil
1½ teaspoons minced fresh parsley
    Pinch of garlic powder
    Pinch of salt

Stir together diced turkey, rice, and vegetables. Whisk vinegar, oil, parsley, and garlic powder together until well blended. Pour over turkey mixture and mix thoroughly. Chill several hours. Stir in salt just before serving to prevent discoloration of vegetables.

Makes six meal-size servings, about 240 calories each.

Turkey Florentine Salad Bowls for Two

4 cups (about 1 pound) washed, torn
    fresh spinach
½ peeled red onion, thinly sliced into
    rings
1 cup sliced raw mushrooms
4 halved cherry tomatoes (or 2 ripe
    tomatoes, diced or sliced into
    wedges)
1 cup (about 5 ounces) diced oven-
    roasted turkey breast fillet
2 tablespoons red-wine vinegar
2 tablespoons liquid pectin
1 tablespoon olive or salad oil
2 tablespoons water
    Pinch of dried oregano
    Salt or garlic salt and pepper to
    taste

Divide spinach between two large salad bowls. Top with onion rings, mushrooms, and tomatoes. Arrange diced turkey over vegetables. Combine remaining ingredients in a covered jar and shake up well. Pour over salads and serve immediately.

Makes two meal-size servings, about 270 calories each.

Japanese Gingered Turkey Salad Bowls

1 torn head Romaine lettuce
1 peeled red onion, sliced into rings
2 ribs celery, thinly sliced on the
    diagonal
1 raw, unpeeled, thinly sliced
    zucchini

Combine vegetables and divide among six salad bowls. Top with turkey and dressing.

Makes six meal-size servings, about 255 calories each.

1 seeded, diced red or green bell
    peppper
½ pound diced turkey ham
½ pound diced oven-roasted turkey
    breast
   Japanese Ginger Dressing (below)

Japanese Ginger Dressing

1 cup low-calorie French salad
    dressing
1 teaspoon ground ginger (or 2
    tablespoons grated fresh ginger
    root or more to taste)
2 tablespoons Japanese-style soy
    sauce
1 minced clove garlic

Combine ingredients in a covered jar. Shake well before serving.

Makes 1⅛ cups, about 22 calories per tablespoon.

Curried Turkey and Mushroom Salad

½ head lettuce, torn into bite-size
    pieces
1 peeled, red onion, sliced into rings
1 seeded, diced green bell pepper
1 cup thinly sliced raw mushrooms
1 cup (about 5 ounces) diced cooked
    turkey or turkey ham
   Curry Cream Salad Dressing
    (p. 142)
2 tablespoons grated Parmesan
    cheese

Line two plates with lettuce and top with onion and pepper rings. Add mushroom slices and cubed turkey. Top with dressings and cheese.

Makes two meal-size servings, about 280 calories each with turkey; 245 calories each with turkey ham.

Curry Cream Salad Dressing

2 tablespoons low-fat mayonnaise
2 tablespoons plain low-fat yogurt or
  sour cream
2 tablespoons low-fat Italian salad
  dressing
3 tablespoons unsweetened apple or
  pineapple juice
½ teaspoon curry powder (or more to
  taste)
  optional: ½ teaspoon sugar or a
  few drops of honey

Stir smooth.

Makes 9 tablespoons, about 12 calories each without sugar; about 13 calories per tablespoon with sugar.

Celery Slaw with Turkey Ham and Apples

3 trimmed, sliced ribs celery
2 unpeeled, diced red apples
¼ cup halved seedless grapes
1 cup (about 5 ounces) cubed turkey
  ham or salami
1 recipe Curry Cream Salad Dressing
  (above)

Combine ingredients and mound on lettuce leaves.

Makes two meal-size servings, about 260 calories each with turkey ham; 295 calories each with turkey salami.

Turkey Ham and Spinach Salad

FOR EACH SERVING:
½ cup diced turkey ham
3 or 4 purple onion rings
½ cup sliced fresh mushrooms
2 cups torn raw spinach
2 tablespoons commercial low-
  calorie French dressing

Arrange ham, mushroom and onion slices on spinach and pour on the dressing.

Makes one serving, about 185 calories.

California Spinach Salad Plates

¾ pound washed raw spinach, stems removed
1 pound low-fat cottage cheese
4 tablespoons grated Parmesan cheese
1 peeled red onion, thinly sliced into rings
4 tablespoons minced fresh parsley
½ pound turkey bologna, cut into julienne strips
12 halved cherry tomatoes
¾ cup low-calorie Italian salad dressing

Line six large salad plates or salad bowls with spinach. Lightly toss together the cottage cheese, Parmesan cheese, onion, and parsley. Mound on each portion of spinach. Add turkey bologna and tomatoes. Top each with two tablespoons salad dressing.

Makes six side-dish servings, about 195 calories each or 3 main-course servings, about 390 calories each.

Meal-Size Macaroni Salad with Turkey Bologna

3 cups tender-cooked protein-enriched elbow macaroni
3 tablespoons low-fat mayonnaise
3 tablespoons lemon juice
3 tablespoons water
1 teaspoon prepared mustard
½ small peeled, finely chopped onion
1 teaspoon celery salt
Pinch of coarsely ground pepper
½ teaspoon dillseed
¼ cup chopped fresh parsley
1 thinly sliced cucumber
2 thinly sliced ribs celery
2 cups (about 10 ounces) diced turkey bologna
Lettuce
2 small ripe tomatoes, cut in wedges

Rinse cooked macaroni in cold water and drain. Stir in remaining ingredients except lettuce and tomato. Arrange on beds of lettuce and top with tomato wedges.

Makes four meal-size servings, about 310 calories each.

Turkey Salami Niçoise

Lettuce
½ pound thinly sliced fresh
   mushrooms
1 thinly sliced cucumber
2 thinly sliced ribs celery
6 halved cherry tomatoes
1 10-ounce package defrosted cut
   green beans (or 1 8-ounce can
   drained, chilled kitchen-cut
   green beans)
1 peeled red onion, thinly sliced into
   rings
3 thinly sliced stuffed green Spanish
   olives
1 pound diced turkey salami
½ cup tomato juice
1 tablespoon lemon juice
1 tablespoon olive oil
1 tablespoon olive juice (from olive
   jar)
Salt and pepper to taste
optional: dash of Worchestershire
   sauce

Line a large salad bowl with lettuce leaves. Arrange vegetables on top and diced turkey salami in the middle. Combine remaining ingredients in covered jar and shake up well to blend. Pour over salad. Serve immediately.

Makes four meal-size servings, about 315 calories each.

Turkey Gazpacho Meal-Size Salad

1 torn head Romaine lettuce
1 peeled, thinly sliced red onion
1 seeded green bell pepper, sliced
   into rings
1 sliced cucumber
2 cups (about 10 ounces) diced
   smoked turkey
4 ripe tomatoes, cut in wedges
¼ cup plain or Bloody Mary-
   seasoned tomato juice
4 tablespoons red-wine vinegar
4 teaspoons olive oil or other salad
   oil
1 minced clove garlic
¼ teaspoon dried oregano
Salt and coarsely ground pepper to
   taste

Line four salad bowls with torn lettuce. Top with sliced onion, pepper, and cucumber. Arrange turkey and tomato on top. Combine remaining ingredients in a covered jar and shake. Pour over salads and serve immediately.

Makes four meal-size servings, about 215 calories each.

Japanese Smoked Turkey Salad Bowl

2 cups (about 10 ounces) diced
  smoked turkey
1 tablespoon Japanese-style soy
  sauce
2 tablespoons sherry
  optional: pinch of ground ginger
  optional: pinch of instant garlic
8 cups chopped lettuce
1 small peeled onion, sliced into
  rings
1½ cups sliced raw mushrooms
½ cup regular or low-calorie French
  dressing

Stir turkey with soy sauce, wine, ginger, and garlic. Cover and chill until serving time.

Combine vegetables and divide among four salad bowls. Drain turkey and arrange over salad. Stir French dressing into remaining marinade and spoon over salads.

Makes four lunch-size servings, about 350 calories each; about 265 calories with low-calorie dressing.

TWELVE ▶ TURKEY WAKER-UPPERS

IF YOU'RE not big on breakfast, here's some food for thought.

For most people there's at least a ten-hour stretch between last night's dinner and this morning's wake-up call. If you're a breakfast skipper the span between yesterday's dinner and today's lunch can add up to an eighteen-hour fast. Not good! Here's why:

According to the U.S. Department of Agriculture (USDA), studies have shown that employees who tuck away a good meal before work get more done than those who skip breakfast or eat a poor one.

Dieters especially lose ground instead of pounds when they try to cut calories by skipping or skimping breakfast. What generally happens is that they succumb to a midmorning "junkfood" break or overeat at lunch. Either way they lose by not losing! Studies have shown that fewer, bigger meals promote weight gain. A dieter does better by dividing calories between breakfast and lunch, instead of spending them all at lunchtime.

In fact, *everyone* is better off with a better breakfast: homemakers, weight watchers, teenagers, laborers, office workers, and executives. Children do better in their schoolwork when they eat a better breakfast.

But the traditional "big" breakfast is especially high in fat, saturated fat, calories, and cholesterol. Many of the menu items uniquely associated with "big" breakfasts are cholesterol- and calorie-rich: eggs, french toast, butter, eggs, bacon, and greasy fried ham.

On the other hand, eat-and-run fast-food breakfasts aren't much better at "breaking-the-fast" than no breakfast. Toast-and-jelly, rolls-and-butter, Danish pastries and sugary cereals are high in empty calories: refined sugar, starch, and fat. The refined carbohydrates give you a quick blast of energy. But it burns out quickly, leaving you even hungrier and less efficient!

The ideal breakfast, according to the USDA, is one that gives you protein, vitamins, and minerals—materials needed to build and repair the body and help keep you healthy.

The best breakfast for anyone who wants to lose weight or avoid gaining is a tasty, balanced menu that includes protein: eggs, low-fat cheese, or lean meat. Eggs and fatty breakfast meats are off-limits for cholesterol watchers. Calorie counters need to avoid traditional breakfast meats like bacon and sausage.

Tips for Trim Breakfast Meats

▶ Today's turkey is a tasty source of trim protein. Because turkey is so lean, turkey breakfast sausage has only a fraction of the fat and calories of traditional pork breakfast sausage: a 2-ounce serving is only 110 calories instead of 282.

▶ Other smoked turkey products are equally at home on the breakfast table. Smoked turkey, turkey ham, pastrami, bologna, and salami can be "pan-fried" in a nonstick skillet with no fat added and served in place of bacon or other fatty pork foods. Even cholesterol watchers can enjoy today's "ham and eggs" by pairing turkey ham with no-cholesterol egg substitute.

Turkey Brunch "Flapjacks"

1 cup (about 5 ounces) diced cooked white-meat turkey
2 eggs (or 4 egg whites or ½ cup defrosted no-cholesterol substitute)
3 slices bread (high-fiber bread may be used)
   optional: pinch of poultry seasoning
1 tablespoon peeled, chopped onion (or 1 teaspoon instant onion)
1 tablespoon fresh parsley
Salt and pepper to taste
2 to 3 tablespoons skim milk

In food processor: Using the steel blade, combine all ingredients except milk and process smooth. Add milk a tablespoon at a time until mixture is the texture of very thick pancake batter.

Without processor: Grind meat, beat eggs, and dice bread. Beat all ingredients together in blender or with electric mixer, adding milk as needed.

Wipe a nonstick skillet lightly with oil or spray with cooking spray for no-fat frying. Heat skillet over moderate flame. Spoon batter onto skillet to make small pancakes. Lower heat and cook until underside is brown, about 3 minutes. Pancakes will not bubble. Turn gently. Cook an additional 3 minutes. Serve with low-fat turkey gravy (p. 168).

Makes six pancakes, about 100 calories each (about 90 calories each with egg whites or egg substitute).

Armenian Turkey Sausage Patties

1 pound turkey breakfast sausage
1 peeled, finely chopped onion
¼ cup finely chopped fresh parsley
  Salt or garlic salt and pepper to
    taste
2 tablespoons lemon juice

Combine ingredients and mix lightly. Shape into eight small patties.

Spray a nonstick skillet with cooking spray for no-fat frying. Add the patties. Cook on one side over moderate heat for 3 to 4 minutes, until underside is well browned. Turn, using a spatula, and brown the other side, an additional 1 or 2 minutes, depending on degree of doneness preferred.

Makes four servings, about 235 calories each.

Italian Pork and Turkey Sausage

1 pound lean ground pork shoulder
1 pound turkey breakfast sausage
  Garlic salt to taste
1 teaspoon mixed Italian seasoning
  optional: ¼ teaspoon red pepper
    flakes
1 tablespoon salad oil

Combine all ingredients except oil. Heat oil in a nonstick skillet, rotating so bottom is evenly coated. Shape mixture into eight flat patties. Cook over low heat, turning once, until cooked through.

Makes eight servings, about 335 calories each.

Broiled or BBQ Pork and Turkey Sausage

Follow recipe for Italian Pork and Turkey Sausage (above), but omit oil. Broil or barbecue patties 3 inches from heat source, until cooked through.

Makes eight servings, about 320 calories each.

Polish Turkey Sausage Patties

1 pound turkey breakfast sausage
1 teaspoon onion powder
1 minced clove garlic (or pinch of
    instant garlic)
½ teaspoon coarse black pepper
1 tablespoon sweet Hungarian
    paprika
½ teaspoon dried marjoram

Combine ingredients. Lightly shape into eight small patties. Broil, bake, or panfry in a nonstick skillet.

Makes eight patties, about 110 calories each.

Turkey Breakfast Ham Slices

1 pound turkey ham

Slice ¼-inch slices from turkey ham. Combine with 2 tablespoons of water in a nonstick skillet. Fry turkey ham over moderate heat, turning once. Serve with favorite breakfast foods: fruit, muffins, eggs.

Makes eight servings, about 80 calories each, turkey ham only.

Turkey Ham 'n' Cheese Strata

4 slices cubed high-fiber bread
2 ounces low-fat American-type diet cheese
2 ounces turkey ham
4 eggs
1 cup skim milk
½ teaspoon prepared mustard
1 tablespoon chopped fresh parsley

Alternate layers of bread, cheese, and turkey ham in a nonstick loaf pan. Combine remaining ingredients and beat well. Pour over strata. Cover with foil. Bake 30 minutes in preheated 350-degree oven, then uncover. Continue to bake until set, an additional 30 minutes or more.

Makes four servings, about 210 calories each.

Baked Turkey Frittata

10 lightly beaten eggs
2 cups (about 10 ounces) diced cooked or smoked turkey or turkey ham
2 seeded, chopped green bell peppers
2 cups peeled, diced ripe tomatoes
1 small peeled, minced onion
2 tablespoons fresh minced parsley (or 2 teaspoons dried parsley)
Salt to taste
optional: 1 teaspoon chili powder
½ teaspoon dried oregano

Note: May be served hot or cold.

Combine ingredients. Spray a nonstick 8-inch square pan or piepan with cooking spray for no-fat baking. Fill with egg mixture. Bake in preheated 350-degree oven for 30 minutes, until set. Cut into wedges to serve.

Makes eight meal-size servings, about 185 calories each; or sixteen appetizers, about 95 calories each.

Turkey Salami-Mushroom Frittata

1 peeled, minced onion
½ pound thinly sliced fresh
   mushrooms
1 teaspoon butter or margarine
1 teaspoon white wine or water
8 lightly beaten eggs (or 2 cups
   defrosted no-cholesterol
   substitute)
  Salt and pepper to taste
1 cup (about 5 ounces) diced turkey
   salami
1 tablespoon chopped fresh parsley

Spray a nonstick skillet or large omelet pan with cooking spray for no-stick frying. Combine onion, mushrooms, butter, and wine. Cook, stirring, over medium heat until liquid evaporates. Pour eggs over mushroom mixture and season with salt and pepper to taste. Sprinkle salami over the eggs. Cover and cook over low heat 10 to 15 minutes, until egg mixture is set. Sprinkle with parsley. Cut into wedges and serve from the skillet.

Makes four servings, about 265 calories each (185 calories each with egg substitute).

Oven-Easy Turkey Foo Yung

2 cups (about 10 ounces) diced
   cooked turkey
2 tablespoons soy sauce
10 lightly beaten eggs (or 2½ cups
   defrosted no-cholesterol
   substitute)
1 16-ounce can rinsed, drained,
   mixed Chinese vegetables
1 peeled, chopped onion
½ seeded, chopped green bell pepper

Combine turkey with soy sauce; mix well. Arrange in bottom of a nonstick 9-inch piepan that has been sprayed with cooking spray for no-fat baking. Combine eggs with remaining ingredients. Spoon over turkey. Bake in preheated 350-degree oven 30 minutes or more, until eggs are set. Cut into wedges to serve.

Makes eight servings, about 185 calories each (135 calories each with egg substitute).

THIRTEEN ▶ TURKEY FOR THE SANDWICH-BORED

Whether you munch a lunch alone at home or brown-bag it to an office, sandwiches can pile on lots of unwanted calories. It's not the bread but the meat of the matter that really adds up. Most "lunchmeats" contain more fat calories than protein. So do hard cheeses. Even skinny seafood fillings become fattening when they're well laced with mayonnaise. Unfortunately, all those extra calories in the middle of your sandwich slide right to your middle!

What's a waistline watcher to do? Sandwiches are such a convenient answer to the what's-for-lunch question, there must be a better alternative to giving them up!

There is. Turkey comes to the rescue when the noon whistle blows. Turkey deli meats are the perfect stand-in for fatty cold cuts. Turkey hot dogs and ground turkey can take the place of ordinary franks and hamburgers, with less fat and fewer calories. Dedicated calorie cutters can save even more by pairing today's trim turkey products with slimmer alternatives when they choose other sandwich ingredients. Here's a guide:

SAVING ON BREAD CALORIES: Choose slim-sliced, high-fiber, diet, protein, or whole-wheat bread over ordinary white bread or rolls. French, Italian, and Middle Eastern pita breads made without added fat (check the label) are also lower in calories than ordinary white breads. Hot dog and hamburger rolls can be "decalorized" by pulling out some of the bread center, leaving just the tasty crust.

151

SAVING ON CHEESE CALORIES: Most natural hard cheeses range between 95 and 115 calories an ounce (Swiss and Cheddar, for example). Part-skim and processed cheeses are lower, 80 calories an ounce and up. Low-fat "diet" cheeses are the least-fattening sliced cheese choices, averaging around 50 calories. (The exact calorie counts will appear on the label.) Low-fat cream cheese and Neufchatel cheese at about 50 to 70 calories an ounce are the low-fat alternatives to cream cheese, which is 105 calories an ounce.

SAVING ON CONDIMENTS: Mustard and horseradish are only 6 calories a tablespoon. Catsup and chili sauce average 18 to 20 calories. But ordinary mayonnaise is a whopping 100 calories . . . or more! Low-fat, low-calorie mayonnaise substitutes are only a fraction of the calories, from 25 to 50 a tablespoon (check the label). Don't forget low-fat, low-calorie "diet" salad dressings as sandwich condiments: Thousand Island and Russian are two favorites.

DON'T FORGET "THE WORKS": Lettuce, tomatoes, pickle chips, dill relish, raw onions, and other sandwich add-ons add more nutrition and appetite appeasement than calories.

Turkey Pizza Hero Sandwiches

FOR EACH SANDWICH:

1 French roll
3 ounces turkey
1 tablespoon chopped ripe olives
2 tablespoons pizza sauce
2 tablespoons shredded part-skim mozzarella cheese
Pinch of dried oregano

Split French roll and remove doughy center. Fill with remaining ingredients.

Wrap each sandwich in plastic wrap. Heat in microwave oven for 30 seconds before serving. Or: Wrap in foil; heat in 250-degree oven 15 to 20 minutes.

Each sandwich, under 430 calories.

Grilled Turkey, Tomato, and Swiss Cheese

2 slices high-fiber bread
2 teaspoons low-calorie mayonnaise
1 ounce sliced Swiss cheese
2 ounces thinly sliced oven-roasted turkey
3 thin slices ripe tomato
optional: 1 teaspoon minced fresh parsley
Celery salt and pepper

Spread bread with mayonnaise. Assemble and grill according to directions for Turkey Pizza Hero Sandwiches (above).

Makes one serving, about 320 calories.

Turkey Joe Steaks-on-a-Roll

2 teaspoons salad oil
4 slices (about ½ pound) raw turkey
    breast
1 peeled, chopped onion
1 seeded, chopped green bell pepper
1 tablespoon prepared mustard
1 tablespoon catsup
    Dash of Worcestershire sauce
1 8-ounce can tomato sauce
2 large hamburger buns, split

Spray a nonstick skillet with cooking spray for no-fat frying. Add the oil and heat over moderate flame. Brown turkey slices quickly on both sides. Add onion, green pepper, mustard, catsup, Worcestershire, and tomato sauce. Cover and simmer until pepper is soft, about 10 minutes. Put a half hamburger bun on each plate. Top each with one turkey slice and sauce. Serve with knives and forks.

    Makes four servings, about 185 calories each.

Texas Herbed Turkey Loaf

2 turkey breast tenderloins (about
    1½ pounds)
1½ cups regular or low-calorie Italian
    dressing
1 cup white wine
½ cup fresh parsley
¼ cup chives or green onion tops
1 minced clove garlic
1 loaf French bread, split lengthwise
1 medium peeled, sliced red onion
1 medium sliced ripe tomato
    Salt and pepper to taste

Marinate tenderloins, covered, in 1 cup salad dressing in the refrigerator all day or overnight.

    In blender mix: ½ cup salad dressing, wine, parsley, chives, and garlic. Spread on split French bread.

    Grill marinated tenderloins over medium-hot coals, 10 minutes per side.

    While turkey is grilling, broil bread halves till golden.

    Remove turkey to platter and slice. Place on bread. Top with onion and tomato season. Place top on bread and secure with long picks. Slice to serve.

    Makes eight servings, about 570 calories each with regular dressing; about 345 calories each with low-calorie dressing.

Greek Pita Pockets

1 pound ground turkey or turkey
    sausage
Pinch of ground cinnamon
Pinch of nutmeg
2 tablespoons lemon juice
1 onion, peeled, halved and thinly
    sliced
1 clove garlic, finely minced
1 large ripe tomato, peeled and
    cubed
2 tablespoons chopped fresh mint (or
    2 teaspoons dried)
½ teaspoon dried oregano
1 tablespoon chopped parsley
½ cup sliced deli-style pickles
    optional: 8 ounces plain lowfat
      yogurt
6 small (or 3 large) pita breads

Shape the meat into tiny meatballs. Brown lightly in a large non-stick skillet which has been sprayed with cooking spray for no-fat frying. Drain and discard fat, if any. Stir in lemon juice, seasonings, onion, pickle and tomato wedges. Cover tightly and simmer 2 to 3 minutes, just until vegetables are heated through but still crisp. Meanwhile, slit pita pockets into half moons. Open to form pockets. Spoon the meat and vegetables into pockets and spoon on yogurt.

Makes six servings, about 300 calories each.

French-Toasted Grilled Turkey Ham 'n' Cheese Sandwiches

1 egg (or ¼ cup defrosted no-
    cholesterol substitute)
3 tablespoons skim milk
4 slices white bread (high-fiber bread
    may be used)
    optional: prepared mustard to taste
2 ounces sliced Swiss cheese or
    white diet cheese
4 ounces sliced turkey ham
Salt and pepper to taste

Beat egg and milk in a shallow bowl. Assemble sandwiches and place in dish. Turn frequently, until egg mixture is absorbed. Lift sandwiches from dish with spatula and place on a nonstick griddle that has been sprayed with cooking spray for no-fat frying. Grill until golden, turning once.

Makes two servings, about 360 calories each, 260 calories each with lower-caloried alternatives.

Dieter's Grilled Turkey Ham 'n' Cheese Sandwich

2 slices high-fiber bread
    optional: prepared mustard to taste
1 ounce sliced extra-sharp American
    Cheddar or diet cheese

Spread bread with mustard, if desired. Put a slice of cheese on top of each slice of bread. Assemble sandwich with remaining ingredients in the middle.

Spray a nonstick skillet or griddle with cooking

2 ounces sliced turkey ham
optional: 3 thin slices ripe tomato

spray for no-fat frying. Put sandwich on cold griddle. Turn heat to moderate. Grill sandwich until underside is golden. Turn sandwich and grill other side.

Makes one serving, about 295 calories with regular cheese; about 230 calories with diet cheese; optional ingredients add about 20 calories.

Curried Turkey Ham Salad Spread

1 cup (about 5 ounces) ground
    turkey ham
1 chopped hard-cooked egg
3 tablespoons minced green bell
    pepper
¼ cup minced celery
2 tablespoons regular or low-fat
    mayonnaise
2 tablespoons unsweetened
    applesauce
½ teaspoon curry powder (or more to
    taste)

Combine ingredients and chill. Serve on salad platter, spread on crackers, or use as sandwich filling.

Makes 1½ cups, about 17 calories per tablespoon with regular mayonnaise; about 15 calories per tablespoon with low-fat mayonnaise.

Grilled Turkey Salami and
Mozzarella Sandwich, Italian Style

2 slices high-fiber bread
1 ounce sliced part-skim mozzarella
    cheese
2 ounces sliced turkey salami
    optional: 3 thin slices ripe tomato
    Pinch of dried oregano or mixed
    Italian seasoning

Assemble and grill according to directions for Turkey Pizza Hero Sandwiches (p. 152).

Makes one serving, about 290 calories (tomato adds about 15 calories).

Grilled Reuben Sandwich

2 thin slices rye bread
    Prepared mustard to taste
1 ounce sliced Swiss cheese
2 ounces sliced turkey pastrami
2 tablespoons well-drained chopped
    sauerkraut

Spread bread with mustard. Assemble and grill according to directions for Turkey Pizza Hero Sandwiches (p. 152).

Makes one serving, about 275 calories.

Relish This Pastrami Sandwich

SPREAD

4 ounces low-calorie cream cheese
1 tablespoon prepared yellow
   mustard
⅓ cup low-calorie Thousand Island
   dressing
6 onion buns, split
12 very thin slices (about 1 pound)
   turkey pastrami
   optional: 6 pitted green olives

Have cream cheese at room temperature. Make spread by combining ingredients. Blend or whip until smooth.

Cover cut surface of each half bun with spread, using about 1 tablespoon per half.

Divide turkey pastrami among sandwiches.

Secure 1 olive on top of each onion bun with a frilled pick, if desired.

Makes six sandwiches, about 205 calories each.

Zesty Mustard Sauce for Turkey Deli Meats

1 cup plain low-fat yogurt
3 to 4 tablespoons horseradish (to
   taste)
¼ cup prepared mustard

Combine in a covered jar and store in refrigerator.

Makes 1½ cups, about 16 calories per tablespoon.

Dilled Cucumber Sauce for Turkey Deli Meats

1 peeled cucumber
1 cup plain low-fat yogurt
1 tablespoon chopped chives
1 teaspoon dillweed
   Salt to taste

Cut cucumber in half. Remove seeds and slice thinly. Combine cucumber, yogurt, chives, dill, and salt. Spread sauce on slices of turkey and either roll up or stack in a bun.

Makes 2 cups, about 6 calories per tablespoon.

FOURTEEN ▸ GREAT ENTERTAINERS

FESTIVE foods needn't be fattening with today's turkey as a hospitality helper. Conventional "party foods" tend to carry a weighty wallop of calories. Cocktail franks, tiny sausages, bacon-wrapped nibbles, creamy dips and cheesey spreads can be a calorie-counter's or cholesterol-watcher's nightmare. Most dinner party dishes and buffet table fare are downright unhospitable to those who watch their waistlines!

You can be the host or hostess with the leastest calories if you use today's turkey and turkey products in place of more fattening alternatives. Turkey deli meats can stand in for the high fat meats usually used in assembling pretty party foods and fancy hors d'oeuvres. Turkey franks and sausages used instead of pork-based products can add a new dimension and sophistication to cocktail trays and party appetizers. Turkey can star in glamorous creations to grace your buffet table when friends come to call. No wonder today's turkey is quickly becoming the beautiful people's party food!

Turkey Party Pâté

A GOOD RECIPE FOR A FOOD PRO-
CESSOR.

2 cups (about 10 ounces) diced
    cooked white-turkey meat
2 peeled hard-cooked eggs
1 tablespoon dry sherry or vermouth
    Salt and pepper to taste
¼ teaspoon chili powder (or to taste)
    Few sprigs fresh parsley
3 or 4 tablespoons low-fat
    mayonnaise

Combine ingredients in food processor, using steel blade, adding just enough mayonnaise to make a paste. Chill until serving time. Serve with crackers.

Makes six appetizer servings, about 115 calories each.

Mrs. Rich's Easy Party Supper

1 turkey breast half (about 2½
    pounds)
    Seasoned salt or garlic salt and
    pepper to taste
1 16-ounce can tomato sauce or
    Marinara or meatless spaghetti
    sauce
½ cup red wine
1 pound sliced fresh mushrooms
½ teaspoon oregano
½ teaspoon basil

Remove skin from breast and discard. Lightly salt and pepper meat. Combine remaining ingredients for sauce. Place breast in a shallow roasting pan and pour sauce over turkey. Cover and roast in preheated 350-degree oven for 1¾ hours, basting occasionally with sauce. (Serve cooked spaghetti as a side dish, if desired.)

Makes eight servings, about 235 calories each. (Tender-cooked spaghetti adds about 155 calories per cupful.)

Easy Turkey Divan

1 tablespoon butter, margarine, or
    diet margarine
1½ pounds turkey breast slices
2 10-ounce packages defrosted
    broccoli spears
1 10-ounce can undiluted Cheddar
    cheese soup
½ cup plain low-fat yogurt
⅛ teaspoon rosemary leaves
    Pinch of paprika

Spray a nonstick skillet with cooking spray for no-fat frying. Melt butter. Sauté turkey slices over high heat just until pink color turns white.

Drain broccoli. Dry with paper towels to remove all additional water.

In a shallow 2-quart baking dish, arrange broccoli, then top with turkey slices. In a bowl blend soup, yogurt, and rosemary. Pour over turkey. Sprinkle with paprika. Bake in preheated 450-degree oven for 15 minutes, or until hot and bubbling.

Makes six servings, about 215 calories each; 210 calories each with diet margarine.

Turkey Jubilee

Follow recipe for Baked Turkey Breast with Cherry Sauce (above). Add 2 tablespoons rum or other high-proof liquor to the simmering cherry sauce. Ignite the vapors with a long match. Spoon flaming sauce over sliced turkey.

Spanish Fruited Turkey Breast

1 turkey breast portion (about 2½ pounds)
1½ cups dry red wine
1 16-ounce can tomatoes
2 peeled, chopped onions
1 seeded, chopped green bell pepper
5 tablespoons golden raisins
¼ cup chopped dried apricots
¼ cup chopped black olives
2 bay leaves
1½ teaspoons dried basil
1 teaspoon thyme
1 teaspoon tarragon

Place the turkey breast portion skin-side up in a shallow, nonstick ovenproof baking dish; bake in preheated 450-degree oven for approximately 20 minutes, until skin is crisp and browned. Pour off any fat.

Combine all remaining ingredients and pour over turkey. Cover loosely with a tent of aluminum foil and lower heat to 350 degrees, so that turkey just simmers. Cook, covered, about 2 hours or more, until turkey is very tender and liquid is reduced to a thick, richly flavored sauce.

Makes eight servings, about 290 calories each.

Baked Turkey Breast with Cherry Sauce

1 turkey breast half (about 2 pounds)
¼ cup dark rum
1 cup undiluted red grape juice
2 tablespoons fresh lemon juice
2 cups fresh, defrosted, pitted sweet red cherries or canned in juice, including juice
½ teaspoon ginger
Salt and pepper to taste
1 tablespoon cornstarch
¼ cup cold water

Bake turkey skin-side up in preheated 450-degree oven for 20 minutes, until skin is crisp. Drain and discard any fat.

Combine rum, grape juice, lemon juice, reserved cherry juice, and ginger; pour over turkey. Add salt and pepper to taste. Cover and bake until turkey is tender, about 1¼ hours; baste frequently with pan juices.

Pour juices into a measuring cup. Skim fat. Add water, if needed, to make 2 cups. Cook, stirring, in a saucepan until boiling. Combine cornstarch and water and stir into simmering sauce until thickened. Add cherries and heat through. Serve with turkey.

Makes six servings, about 305 calories each.

Turkey Fillets and Mushrooms

½ cup dry sherry or other white wine
1 tablespoon salad oil
1 pound raw turkey breast slices
½ pound sliced fresh mushrooms
   Salt and freshly ground pepper

Put 2 tablespoons of the wine in a nonstick skillet; add oil and turkey. Heat over high flame until wine evaporates and turkey slices begin to brown in remaining melted fat. When steaks are brown on one side, turn them over and add mushrooms. Cook an additional 3 to 4 minutes, until mushrooms are lightly browned. Remove to a heated platter. Add remaining wine to skillet. Cook, stirring, until wine is bubbling; season to taste, and pour over turkey.

Makes four servings, about 190 calories each.

Turkey Steaks au Poivre (PEPPERCORN STEAK)

2 or 3 teaspoons whole peppercorns
1 pound turkey breast tenderloin
   steaks
1 tablespoon salad oil

Use a mortar and pestle to coarsely crack the fresh peppercorns. (Or put the whole peppercorns in a plastic bag and pound with a hammer.) Press cracked pepper into both sides of steaks. Refrigerate 1 hour or more.

Spray a nonstick skillet with cooking spray for no-fat frying, then add oil and heat. Add steaks and cook quickly on both sides, until cooked through. Remove steaks to a serving dish and sprinkle lightly with Worcestershire, Tabasco, or lemon juice. Garnish with parsley and lemon wedges.

Makes four servings, about 165 calories each.

Mrs. Rich's Turkey in Ambrosia Sauce

1 turkey hindquarter (about 3½
   pounds)
   Garlic salt and pepper to taste
1 cup fat-skimmed turkey broth or
   water
¾ cup port wine
2 teaspoons steak or Worcestershire
   sauce
1 teaspoon catsup
6 tablespoons dried currants or
   raisins

Season hindquarter with garlic salt and pepper; place skin-side up on a nonstick baking pan. Bake in preheated 450-degree oven 20 to 25 minutes, until skin is crisp. Drain and discard any fat. Combine broth, wine, steak sauce, catsup, currants, optional peel, and spices and pour over turkey. Add juice from canned cherries and oranges. Lower heat to 350 degrees. Bake, uncovered, basting frequently with sauce, until turkey is tender, about 1¼ to 1½ hours.

Drain sauce from roasting pan into a saucepan.

optional: ¼ teaspoon grated orange peel

pinch of ground cloves, ground nutmeg, thyme, and allspice

1 16-ounce can undrained, juice-packed pitted sweet red cherries

1 8-ounce can undrained, juice-packed mandarin oranges

2 teaspoons cornstarch

¼ cup cold water

Surround turkey with drained cherries and oranges. Cover with foil and return to oven, just until fruit is heated through.

Meanwhile, skim fat from the surface of sauce with a bulb-type baster. Heat to boiling. Combine cornstarch with cold water and stir into simmering sauce. Cook, stirring, until sauce is thick. To serve, slice turkey and serve with fruit and sauce.

Makes ten servings, about 395 calories each.

Stuffed Turkey Thighs Florentine

½ cup peeled, chopped onion

1 minced clove garlic

½ teaspoon mixed Italian seasoning

1 tablespoon butter, margarine, or diet margarine

1 large beaten egg (or 2 egg whites or ¼ cup defrosted no-cholesterol susbtitute)

½ cup chopped, cooked spinach

½ cup fine, soft bread crumbs

½ cup grated Parmesan cheese

Salt and pepper to taste

2 turkey thighs (about 3 pounds)

Sauté onion, garlic, and herbs in butter until soft but not browned. Combine eggs, spinach, bread crumbs, cheese, salt, and pepper. Add onion mixture and mix well. Set aside.

With a sharp-pointed knife, bone turkey thighs by cutting down to bone on inside of thigh; then cut meat carefully away from bone. Pound meat out to flatten as much as possible.

Divide the filling mixture between the two flattened turkey thighs. Bring skin together to enclose filling, and skewer or tie with string. Skewer ends of rolls. Wrap loosely in foil. Place on shallow baking pan. Bake in preheated 350-degree oven for 1 hour. Open foil and bake 1 hour longer, until meat is tender and rolls are nicely browned. Remove skewers. Cut into slices to serve. Serve warm or cold.

Makes ten servings, about 340 calories each (330 calories each with diet margarine and egg whites or egg substitute).

Turkey Thigh Kebabs Teriyaki

1 turkey thigh (about 1½ pound)
⅓ cup soy or bottled teriyaki sauce
¼ cup water or juice from pineapple
2 seeded green bell peppers, cut into
    1-inch squares
4 small peeled, halved onions
1 cup drained, juice-packed
    pineapple chunks

Debone and skin turkey thigh and cut meat into 1-inch cubes. Discard bones and skin.

Combine turkey cubes with cooking marinade: soy sauce and water. Cover and simmer over low heat until meat is tender, about 1 hour. (Add water, if needed.) Allow to cool. Thread meat on skewers, alternating with pepper, onion, and pineapple. Brush well with remaining pan juices. Broil or barbecue, turning frequently and brushing with marinade, just until green pepper is tender-crisp.

Makes five servings, about 335 calories each.

Turkey Thigh Veronique

1 turkey thigh
¼ cup dry white wine
¾ cup fat-skimmed turkey or chicken
    broth
    Salt and pepper to taste
    optional: pinch of ground nutmeg
1 cup skim milk
2 tablespoons flour
1 cup seedless grapes (or 4
    tablespoons golden raisins)

Note: To heat grapes: Put them in a wire strainer and lower strainer into pan of hot water for 2 to 3 minutes. Drain.

Spray a nonstick skillet, Dutch oven, or ovenproof casserole with cooking spray for no-fat frying. Put thigh skin-side down in skillet. Add 2 tablespoons wine and cook slowly over low flame until wine evaporates and turkey browns in its own melted fat. Cook until skin is crisp and well rendered of fat. Drain and discard any fat.

Turn turkey skin-side up and add remaining ingredients except milk, flour, and grapes. Cover and simmer until tender, 1½ hours or more. Uncover and continue to cook until most of the liquid evaporates.

Stir milk and flour together, then stir into the simmering skillet over low heat until sauce thickens and bubbles. (Thin with water, if needed.) Garnish with heated grapes.

Makes five servings, about 325 calories each.

Turkey Nut Balls

1 cup ground cooked turkey
3 tablespoons low-fat mayonnaise
1½ tablespoons grated onion
½ teaspoons celery salt
　Dash of pepper
2 tablespoons minced parsley
3 drops Tabasco
3 tablespoons finely chopped walnuts

Combine all ingredients except nuts. Mix well and chill. Shape into large individual ball or into small bitesize pieces; roll in the nuts. Cover and chill until serving time. Serve plain or with crisp crackers or vegetables.

　Makes fifteen servings, about 35 calories each.

Turkey-Stuffed Cabbage Rolls

1 medium head green cabbage

FILLING

1 pound ground turkey
　Salt and pepper to taste
1 peeled, minced onion
2 tablespoons chopped fresh parsley
1 lightly beaten egg (or 2 egg whites
　　or ¼ cup defrosted no-
　　cholesterol substitute)
1 cup cooked rice
1 tablespoon Worcestershire sauce

SAUCE

1 20-ounce can chopped tomatoes
2 tablespoons cider vinegar
¼ cup apple juice or cider
3 tablespoons catsup
1 tablespoon cornstarch
　Garlic salt and pepper to taste

Cut cabbage in quarters and remove core. Separate leaves. Drop in boiling water just long enough to soften cabbage.

　Combine filling ingredients and mix thoroughly. Spoon some filling into each cabbage leaf and roll up, tucking in ends.

　Arrange the rolls in a large skillet or heavy pot. Add tomatoes and vinegar. Cover and simmer over low heat for 1 hour. Remove rolls to a serving dish. Combine apple juice, catsup, and cornstarch; stir into simmering tomatoes, until slightly thickened. Season to taste and pour over cabbage rolls.

　Makes six servings, about 240 calories each.

Turkey Teriyaki Meatballs

1 pound ground turkey
optional: ½ teaspoon MSG
Salt and pepper to taste
⅛ teaspoon ground ginger
¼ cup peeled, chopped onion (or 4
    teaspoons instant onion)
¼ cup chopped celery
½ cup unseasoned bread crumbs
1 egg (or 2 egg whites or ¼ cup
    defrosted no-cholesterol
    substitute)
¼ cup soy sauce
¼ cup sherry or other dry white wine
¼ cup defrosted, undiluted pineapple
    juice concentrate
1 teaspoon ground ginger
2 cups fat-skimmed turkey broth
2 tablespoons cornstarch

Combine ground turkey, optional MSG, salt, pepper, ginger, onion, celery, bread crumbs, and egg. Shape into 1-inch balls. Place on rack in shallow pan. Bake in preheated 400-degree oven for 10 to 12 minutes.

In a nonstick saucepan combine soy sauce, wine, juice, ginger, broth, and cornstarch. Cook, stirring, over moderate heat, until boiling. Cook over medium heat, stirring often, for 5 minutes. Add meatballs and heat through. (Serve meatballs over noodles or rice, if desired, or transfer to a heated chafing dish as a party appetizer.)

Makes forty meatballs, about 36 calories each; or four main-course servings, about 360 calories each (350 calories each serving with egg whites or egg substitute). (Each ½ cup tender-cooked noodles or fluffy rice adds about 100 calories.)

Terrific Turkey Rolls

3 ounces sliced cooked ham or
    turkey ham
3 ounces sliced part-skim mozzarella
    cheese
6 (about 1 pound) turkey breast
    slices
½ teaspoon sage
1 medium diced ripe tomato
⅓ cup dry unseasoned bread crumbs
2 tablespoons Parmesan cheese
2 tablespoons snipped fresh parsley
4 tablespoons regular Italian salad
    dressing

Place half slice of ham and mozzarella on each turkey slice. Top with sage and tomato. Roll and secure with toothpicks.

Combine bread crumbs, Parmesan cheese, and parsley. Dip turkey rolls in salad dressing and roll in crumb mixture. Place in a shallow baking dish and bake for 20 minutes in preheated 350-degree oven.

Makes six servings, about 220 calories each.

Salami Cornucopias

2 ounces crumbled blue or Roquefort
    cheese
2 ounces part-skim ricotta cheese
16 slices (about 8 ounces) turkey
    salami

Blend cheeses. Spread each salami slice with 1 tablespoon mixture. Roll into a cornucopia.
    Makes sixteen, about 45 calories each.

Turkey Ham and Cheese Logs

16 slices process Swiss cheese or
    white diet cheese (8 ounces)
16 slices hickory-smoked turkey ham
    slices (8 ounces)

Center cheese slice on turkey ham slice; roll and secure with picks. (Pickle spear may be rolled inside, if desired.)
    Makes sixteen servings, about 75 calories each with regular cheese; about 45 calories each with diet cheese.

Turkey Pinwheels

8 ounces low-fat cream cheese or
    Neufchatel
4 tablespoons skim milk or plain
    yogurt
1 teaspoon horseradish (to taste)
1 pound sliced turkey pastrami or
    bologna

Whip cheese with milk and horseradish until spreadable. Spread cheese mixture evenly on pastrami or bologna slices and roll up; secure with picks if necessary. Cover and chill thoroughly. Slice each roll into one-inch lengths. Garnish with cherry tomatoes, olives, and parsley, if desired.
    Makes twenty-four appetizers, about 45 calories each with turkey pastrami; about 60 calories each with turkey bologna.

Curried Fruited Turkey Franks

¾ cup (16-ounce can) tomato juice
1 12 ounce can unsweetened apricot
  or peach nectar
¼ cup golden raisins
4 small peeled, quartered onions
1 seeded, cubed red or green bell
  pepper
  optional: pinch of garlic powder
1¼ teaspoons curry powder
1 pound (10) turkey frankfurters,
  sliced into 1-inch lengths
1 cored, diced, unpeeled red apple

Combine all ingredients except franks and apple in a large nonstick skillet. Simmer, uncovered, stirring occasionally, about 10 minutes (just until onions and pepper are crunchy and liquid is reduced to a thick sauce).

Stir franks and apple into skillet at the last minute. Cook only until heated through.

Makes four servings, about 380 calories each.

Turkey Franks in a Blanket

5 turkey franks
3 large crisp new pickles
10 ready-to-bake refrigerated biscuits
  (1 8-ounce tube can)

Slice franks into quarters lengthwise, and then in half crosswise, making each into 8 strips. Cut the pickles into 40 slivers of approximately the same size as the franks.

Roll or pat each biscuit section into a long, thin oval; cut in 2 lengthwise pieces, then crosswise forming 4 thin strips of dough from each.

Roll 1 frank strip and 1 pickle strip in each cut piece of dough, forming a band around the middle. Seal the edges of the dough. Place each bundle on a nonstick cookie sheet, sprayed with cooking spray for no-fat baking, with the sealed edge down.

Bake in preheated 450-degree oven 10 to 12 minutes, or until the dough is golden brown. Serve with mustard for dipping.

Makes 40 franks in blankets, about 35 calories each.

Cold Smoked Turkey Kebabs

1 large cubed cucumber
30 cherry tomatoes
1 pound smoked turkey breast, cut
  into ¾-inch cubes

Skewer turkey alternately with a cube of cucumber and a cherry tomato. Cover serving platter with Romaine, endive, or bibb lettuce. Top with skewers.

Makes thirty appetizers, about 25 calories each.

FIFTEEN ▶ TURKEY FOR THE HOLIDAYS

YOU DON'T NEED to wait for a crowd to gather to declare a turkey holiday. Today's versatile turkey is available in forms to turn any event into a festive celebration, no matter what the date. Or the number attending.

Turkey, of course, is traditional for Thanksgiving and Christmas celebrations. But with today's smaller families and hectic life styles, it's not always possible or practical to stuff and roast a big bird. Yet these holidays just aren't the same without turkey *and* all the trimmings.

You can still enjoy "turkey with all the trimmings" *without* the usual work—and all those leftovers—even if your holiday table is set for only a few places. A roast turkey breast—or breast half or hindquarter—is just the right size for the smaller family.

You can scale down the menu in calories, too. Dressings can be made in a casserole, with more vegetables and less bread, and no fat added. Delicious turkey gravy can be virtually fat-free. Traditional vegetables can be cooked in turkey broth, no butter needed. Fresh cranberry sauce can be whipped up in a blender with more fruit and less sugar. Even the traditional desserts can be calorie-edited to provide more nutrition with less sugar, fat, and starch.

In this section we've put festive, nonfattening recipes that are easy to prepare—to help you combine tradition with today's demands. We've also included "special occasion" turkey dishes for any time of year.

Gravy Without Fat

Don't most diet plans rule out gravies? Yes, and with good reason: Conventional gravies usually harbor unneeded calories in the form of fat and oil. It's the fat, not the thickeners, that thicken waistlines needlessly! You can get rid of unneeded calories from gravy simply by skimming the fat from the broth or pan drippings that serve as the base. You can defat any sauce simply by omitting the fat or fatty ingredients called for in conventional recipes. Use these rules to sauce up holiday turkey:

▶ Before making gravy, drain the pan juices into a jar or measuring cup. Scrape up the flavorful residue from the roasting pan by adding a little hot water. Wait till the fat rises to the surface, then remove it with your bulb baster. (Or, chill the juices until the fat hardens on top; then lift it off.)

▶ Measure the stock, then add water to make the amount of gravy you want. Reheat it in a saucepan.

▶ For each cup of gravy wanted, stir 2 tablespoons flour into ¼ cup cold water. Stir the paste into the simmering liquid.

▶ Simmer the gravy until thick. If it becomes too thick, thin it with a little water. Season to taste with salt and pepper or vary the flavor with herbs. (MSG will intensify the taste of a weak gravy, but some people are allergic to it.) For a darker gravy, add a little soy sauce or brown gravy base. Sprinkle with chopped fresh parsley before serving.

Gravy without drippings can be made from fat-skimmed turkey broth made from necks or wings (see page 126). Or, you may substitute canned, condensed chicken broth. (First, skim the globules of fat from the surface.) Combine a 10¼-ounce can, undiluted, with 3 tablespoons flour. Cook, stirring, until thick; then season to taste. Or use homemade fat-skimmed broth simmered from leftover bones. Or a broth reconstituted with boiling water and bouillon cubes or concentrated beef stock.

Low-calorie "cream" gravy can be made by substituting skim milk for part of the water. Before making the gravy, fat-skim the pan juices and simmer them down to a rich concentrate. Combine cold liquid skim milk with flour. Blend well, then stir into the saucepan. Cook, stirring, over low heat until thick. Add seasonings and herbs to taste.

Stuffing or Dressing Without Fat

Fat isn't a necessary ingredient in dressing, so you can "decalorize" any favorite combination simply by following these suggestions:

▶ Omit the oil, butter, or other fats called for in a recipe.

▶ It's not necessary to prefry chopped onions, celery, or other vegetables added to dressing combinations.

▶ The broth or pan drippings used to moisten dressing should be fat-skimmed before being added to the mixture.

▶ If your favorite recipe includes sausage meat, you can substitute the lower-fat turkey sausage and save considerable calories.

▶ If you are using a packaged stuffing mix and the directions call for the addition of butter or fat, simply omit it!

High-Fiber, Lower-Calorie Dressing

To increase the fiber in your favorite combination, try some of these suggestions:

▶ Substitute high-fiber bread for ordinary white bread.

▶ Increase the ratio of vegetables to bread: more onions and celery, a little less bread.

▶ Because vegetables have a high moisture content, decrease the amount of liquid called for. Decrease the liquid by ½ cup for each additional cupful of chopped vegetables.

▶ Follow the preceding suggestions for cutting down on fat.

High-Fiber Bread Dressing

10 slices high-fiber bread
½ cup fat-skimmed turkey broth
1 cup chopped celery
1 cup peeled, chopped onion
¼ cup chopped fresh parsley
1 teaspoon mixed poultry seasoning
   Salt and pepper to taste
   optional: 1 or 2 tablespoons dry
      white wine

Dice bread into cubes. Toss lightly with remaining ingredients. Spoon mixture into a nonstick baking pan or casserole. Cover and bake 45 minutes at 350 degrees, or 1 hour at 325 degrees. (Double the recipe for "stuffing.")

Makes six servings, about 100 calories each.

Protein-Enriched Turkey Dressing Casserole

2 cups skim milk
3 eggs
2 peeled, minced onions
3 minced ribs celery
1 minced clove garlic
2 cups seasoned stuffing mix
   Salt and pepper to taste

Scald milk and allow it to cool. Add eggs and fork-whip lightly. Mix in onion, celery, garlic and stuffing mix. Season to taste. Spoon into a nonstick loaf pan or ovenproof casserole. Bake at 325 degrees for 50 minutes, until set.

Makes eight servings, about 125 calories each.

VARIATIONS: Add a ½ cup of drained canned mushrooms (10 calories) or cooked minced turkey giblets and more low-fat protein (less than 60 calories an ounce). For individual servings, pile the mixture into nonstick muffin pans and cut the baking time to 30 minutes.

OR: Use two cups of cubed high-fiber bread instead of the packaged stuffing mix. If the bread is fresh, toast it lightly before cutting it into cubes. Add a teaspoon of mixed poultry seasoning.

IN A HURRY?: Use 1 cup evaporated skim milk and 1 cup water instead of the 2 cups scalded milk. Two tablespoons of dried onion flakes and a tablespoon of dried celery can serve as a stand-in for the minced vegetables. Season with garlic powder and salt.

Rangetop Mushroom "Dressing"

½ pound finely chopped fresh
      mushrooms
1 cup shredded carrots
1 cup diced celery

In a nonstick saucepan, combine mushrooms with remaining ingredients. Over low heat, cover and cook 30 minutes or longer, stirring occasionally. Serve hot.

¾ cup peeled, minced onion
½ cup fat-skimmed turkey broth
1 tablespoon chopped fresh parsley
  Salt and pepper to taste
¼ teaspoon poultry seasoning
  optional: 2 tablespoons dry sherry

Makes about 2 cups (four servings), about 45 calories each serving.

Spiced Acorn Squash

Acorn squashes
Undiluted, defrosted orange juice
  concentrate
Fat-skimmed turkey broth
Salt, pepper, and pumpkin pie
  spice to taste

Cut each squash in half and scoop out the seeds. Place halves cut-side up in a shallow roasting pan. Place 1 tablespoon orange juice concentrate in the center of each squash and fill the cavity with fat-skimmed turkey broth. Sprinkle with salt, pepper, and pumpkin pie spice. Bake, uncovered, in a 325- or 350-degree oven until squash is fork-tender. To serve, divide each squash half in two sections lengthwise.

Each serving (¼ squash), about 55 calories.

Turkey Mashed Turnip

4 cups diced yellow turnip (rutabaga)
  (fresh or frozen)
1 cup fat-skimmed turkey broth
  Salt and pepper to taste

In a saucepan combine ingredients. Cover and simmer 10 to 15 minutes, until turnip is tender. Mash without draining, using a potato masher or electric mixer.

Makes six servings, about 50 calories each.

Savory Stuffed Turkey Breast Half

1 turkey breast half (about 2½ pounds)
1 cup sliced fresh mushrooms
½ cup chopped celery
½ cup seeded, chopped green bell pepper
¼ cup chopped fresh parsley
¼ cup peeled, chopped onion
2 cups fat-skimmed turkey or chicken broth
1 cup raw rice
½ teaspoon dried marjoram
¼ teaspoon garlic powder
½ teaspoon summer savory
Salt and pepper to taste

Bake turkey skin-side up in preheated 450-degree oven, until skin is crisp. Drain and discard any fat. Combine remaining ingredients in the bottom of a covered baking dish. Place browned breast half over the filling, skin-side up. Salt and pepper to taste. Lower heat to 325 degrees, cover, and bake about 2 hours, until tender.

Makes nine servings, about 275 calories each.

Low-Calorie High-fiber Bread Dressing with Apples and Raisins

10 slices high-fiber bread, stale or toasted
4 peeled, quartered onions
optional: 2 cloves garlic (or ¼ teaspoon instant garlic)
optional: ¼ cup dry white wine
6 trimmed ribs celery
4 unpeeled, quartered, cored cooking apples
1 cup fresh parsley
1¼ cups fat-skimmed turkey or chicken broth (homemade or canned)
½ cup raisins
Salt and pepper to taste
1 teaspoon mixed poultry seasoning or sage (or more, to taste)
½ teaspoon cinnamon
¼ teaspoon nutmeg

With blender or food processor (using steel blade): Process bread into crumbs a few slices at a time. Combine onions, optional garlic, and wine; add to blender and chop coarsely with quick on-off motions. Chop celery, apples, and parsley by hand. Combine all ingredients.

By hand: Put bread in a plastic bag a few slices at a time. Crush with a rolling pin. Continue until all bread is crushed. Chop onions and celery. Dice apples. Mince parsley and garlic. Combine all ingredients.

Toss ingredients lightly. Spray a shallow roasting pan with cooking spray for no-fat baking and fill with dressing. Cover with foil and bake 1 hour in preheated 325-degree oven. Or use to stuff turkey.

Makes twelve servings, about 110 calories each.

Orange-Cranberry-Raisin Relish for Poultry, Pork, or Ham

1 unpeeled, seedless eating orange
1 cup fresh raw cranberries
1 cup golden raisins

Quarter orange and process in a blender or food processor (using steel blade) with quick on-off motions until coarsely chopped. Add cranberries and process until chopped. Add raisins and process with two or three quick on-off motions, just until mixed. Store in refrigerator.

Makes 3 cups, about 10 calories per tablespoon.

Easter Sunday Roast Turkey Hindquarter

1 young turkey hindquarter (3 to 4 pounds)
4 tablespoons lemon juice
2 teaspoons dried oregano or rosemary
optional: 1 teaspoon dried mint
optional: ⅛ teaspoon instant garlic
Salt and pepper to taste

Arrange turkey skin-side up on rack in shallow roasting pan. Sprinkle liberally with lemon juice, herbs, and seasonings. Insert a meat thermometer into the deepest part of the meat, not touching the bone. Place roast in a cold oven, then set temperature gauge at 300 degrees. Roast, uncovered, basting occasionally with additional lemon juice, until meat thermometer registers 185 degrees. Do not overcook. Allow to stand 10 to 20 minutes before carving.

Each four-ounce serving, about 335 calories.

Double-Berry Cranberry Sauce

4 cups fresh raw cranberries
2 cups water
1 4-serving envelope strawberry, raspberry, or cherry gelatin (regular or sugar-free)

Combine cranberries and water in a large saucepan. Cover and simmer over very low heat until cranberries have popped open. Remove from heat and add gelatin, stirring until completely dissolved. Pour in covered jar and chill in refrigerator until set.

Makes ten servings, about 50 calories each with regular gelatin; about 25 calories with sugar-free gelatin.

Oven Cranberry Sauce

2 cups fresh raw cranberries
2 tablespoons water

Wash cranberries and combine with water in a covered casserole. Bake in preheated 325-degree oven for 30 minutes, or until berries pop open.

Makes four servings, about 40 calories each without sweetener. (Sweeten to taste with a few drops honey, if desired.)

Raw Cranberry-Orange Relish

2 cups fresh raw cranberries
1 sweet eating orange
1 cup white raisins

In blender, grinder, or food processor (using steel blade): Chop up the cranberries. Peel and cut up the orange, removing any seeds. Add the orange and half the peel to container and chop. Stir in raisins by hand. Chill before serving.

Makes eight servings, about 75 calories each.

Pineapple-Spiced Cranberry Sauce I

3 cups fresh raw cranberries
1 6-ounce can defrosted, undiluted pineapple juice or cider concentrate
6 tablespoons golden raisins
  optional: pinch of pumpkin pie spice

In a saucepan, combine ingredients and simmer over very low heat, just until cranberries pop open. Chill before serving.

Makes eight servings, about 85 calories each.

Pineapple-Spiced Cranberry Sauce II

1 16-ounce can juice-packed crushed pineapple
4 cups fresh raw cranberries
½ teaspoon pumpkin pie spice

In a saucepan, combine and simmer over very low heat, just until cranberries pop open. Chill.

Makes sixteen servings, about 30 calories each.

Pumpkin Custard

2 cups cooked or canned
    unsweetened pumpkin
4 eggs
¾ cup skim milk
¾ cup honey
4 tablespoons all-purpose flour
¼ teaspoon salt
2 teaspoons vanilla extract
1½ teaspoons pumpkin pie spice

Beat ingredients together in electric mixer bowl or blender. Pour into baking dish. Place the dish in a larger baking dish containing 1 inch of boiling water. Place in preheated 400-degree oven and bake 1 hour, until a knife inserted in the center comes out clean. Chill before serving.

Makes eight servings, about 175 calories each.

Index

À la India, 37
Acorn squash, spiced, 171
Adobo, 34
Almonds, 68
Aloha, 122–123
Ambrosia sauce, 160–161
Apples, 119, 142, 172
Applesauce, 86
Apricot sauce, 44
Armenian turkey sausage patties, 148
Au vin rouge, 71

Barbecue sauces, 51
   Chinese style, 94
   for cut-up parts, 96
   fat-free, 95
   ginger, 100
   Mexican, 94–95
Barbecuing and broiling, 92–93
Bavarian meatballs, 38–39
Beans:
   green, 41, 76, 77, 79, 134
   lima, 36
   lima bean chili, 74
Bisque, 129
Blender loaf, 60–61
Blue Ribbon, 51
Bologna (see Turkey bologna)
Bouillon cubes, frozen, 127
Bread dressing, high fiber, 170
   with apples and raisins, 172
Breaded patties, Swedish, 41
Breakfast, 146–147
Breast Adelphi, 48–49
Breast, baked, with cherry sauce,
   158–159
Breast, cider-baked, 49
Breast, "Georgian Style," 50
Breast half, savory stuffed, 172
Breast with herbs, foil-baked, 48
Breast, Mediterranean with olives, 81
Breast, Mexican fruited, 81
Breast, Polynesian barbecue portion, 96
Breast, Spanish fruited, 159
Breast steaks, Chinese broiled, 99
Breast Valenciana, 50

Broccoli, 68, 134–135
   Primavera, 124
Broiling and barbecuing, 92–93
Burger (see Turkeyburger)

Cabbage, 77
Cabbage rolls, stuffed, 163
Cacciatore, one-pan, 124
California spinach salad plates, 143
Calories, 8–9, 30–31, 66, 80, 92–93, 105,
   125, 138, 146–147, 151–152, 157,
   167–169
   comparative charts, 11–13
Cantonese, 33
Carbonnade, 86
Carrots, 130
   compote, 135
   in wine sauce, 135
Cashews, 46
   cashew curry, 67
Casino marinade, 94
Casino wingettes, 57
Cauliflower au gratin, 136
Celery slaw with turkey ham and apples,
   142
Cheddar-baked zucchini and turkey ham,
   64
Cheese, 33, 39, 70–71, 84, 102, 113, 149,
   151, 152, 154–155, 165
Cheese loaf, 60
Cheeseburgers, 116
Cherries, 54
Cherry sauce, 158–159
Chili:
   eggplant, 91
   with rice, 122
   con turkey, 106
   Texas turkey, 88
   turkey–lima bean, 74
Chinatown, 68
Chinese broiled breast steaks, 99
Chinese pepper skillet for two, 113
Chinese-style barbecue sauce, 94
Cholesterol, 8, 9, 11
Chop suey, smoked, 77
Chow mein, speedy skillet, 67

Relish: cranberry, raisin, orange, 173, 174
Reuben sandwich, grilled, 155
Rice, 122, 136
Rich, Louis, 13
Risotto, 112
Roast hindquarter, 173
Roast, Israeli, tarragon, 32
Roast, "Waikiki," 89
Rockwell, Norman, 16, 17
Rolled thighs with cherries, 54
Roquefortburgers, 102
Rouladen, 32

Sahara thigh with zucchini, 54
Salad, 138
  California spinach, 143
  celery slaw with turkey ham and
    apples, 142
  curried turkey and mushroom, 141
  dressing, curry cream, 142
  Florentine, 140
  gazpacho, 144
  Japanese gingered, 140–141
    dressing, 141
  Japanese smoked, 145
  macaroni, 139
    and turkey bologna, 143
  orchard, marinated, 139
  turkey ham and spinach, 142
  turkey salami Nicoise, 144
  vinaigrette, 140
  Waldorf, 139
Salami (*see* Turkey salami)
Salami sauce, 44
Sandwiches, 151–152
  Greek pita pockets, 154
  ham and cheese, dieter's, grilled,
    154–155
  ham and cheese, French-toasted,
    grilled, 154
  ham salad spread, curried, 155
  pastrami, 156
  pizza hero, 152
  Reuben, grilled, 155
  salami and mozzarella, grilled, Italian
    style, 155

Sandwiches (*con't*)
  sauces, 156
  steaks-on-a-roll, 153
  Swiss cheese and tomato, grilled, 152
  Texas herbed loaf, 153
Sauces:
  ambrosia, 160–161
  apricot, 44
  barbecue, 51
  cherry, 158–159
  cranberry, 173–174
  "cream," 53, 82
  dilled cucumber for turkey deli meats,
    156
  "imitation" sour cream, 64–65
  mustard, for turkey deli meats, 156
  plum, 87
  salami, 44
  savory tomato, 52
  Spanish, 58
  spice, 56
  turkey meat for pasta, 89
  turkeyburger, 116
  white, 48
  wine, 112, 135
  (*see also* Barbecue)
Sauerkraut, 76, 90
Sausage (*see* Turkey sausage)
Sausage patties, spicy, Italian, 75
Savory stuffed breast half, 172
Savory tomato sauce, 52
Savory turkey loaf, 63
Savory turkeyburgers, 102
Seasonings and spices, 30
Shopper's guide, 3–6
Skewered, 97, 98, 119
Skillet Stroganoff, 67
Slimming, 9
Smoked chop suey, 77
Smoked turkey products, 6, 26, 147
Smothered tidbits, 69
Soup, 125–126
  base, 126
  basic turkey-vegetable, 127
  bisque, 129
  cock-a-leekie, 132